Everyday Self-Defense

Everyday Self-Defense

Protect yourself with attitude, intuition and strategy

KHALEGHL QUINN

Thorsons
An Imprint of HarperCollins*Publishers*

Thorsons
An imprint of HarperCollins*Publishers*
1160 Battery Street
San Francisco, California 94111-1213
77–85 Fulham Palace Road,
Hammersmith, London W6 8JB

Published by Thorsons as
Khaleghl Quinn's Art of Self-Defence 1993
This USA edition published 1994
10 9 8 7 6 5 4 3 2 1

A catalogue record for this book
is available from the British Library

ISBN 0 7225 2991 0

Phototypeset by Harper Phototypesetters Limited,
Northampton, England
Printed in Great Britain by
Woolnough Bookbinding, Irthlingborough, Northants

I

This book is dedicated to all the women and children of the world.

II

This book is dedicated to all the men in the world who have done their best to diminish the fear and personal insecurities in other men that leads them to cowardly violence against those of lesser physical strength than them. This book is also dedicated to the men who fight violence for reasons deeper than just basic decency.

III

This book is especially dedicated to Olympic gold medalist, Hassiba Boulmerka of Algeria, an individual who has exhibited great courage, inner strength and tremendous hard work in the face of a culture which does not necessarily approve of women developing themselves through sport. Her disciplined spirit should easily project her as a beacon of unrelenting inspiration. By her living example, she epitomizes the quintessential meaning of this book.

Contents

1 | **The First Dimension**

THE REALM OF AWARENESS

HOW TO USE THIS BOOK

There are many books written about the martial arts with an increasing emphasis on self-defence. The focus varies: some are technical martial arts manuals, others apply these techniques in a martial arts mode, and still others are geared towards assertiveness.

When our unique needs as individuals are taken into account, the topic of self-defence as a response to the varying degrees of violence in the world becomes a complex issue. Taking up a martial art or relying on the advice, 'Just use common sense', that was the prevalent, over-simplified approach of twenty years ago, is no longer enough. To feel more secure in the world we need a reliable variety of appropriate responses and techniques to call upon in threatening situations.

I hope that this book will serve as an organising tool to further distil and elucidate the potential of the martial arts and, furthermore, as a means to harnessing and directing our individual life forces in the most practical, appropriate and fulfilling ways. I feel that in order to accomplish this aim we must get to the root of violence, the very need for self-defence. This book is intended to provide a comprehensive strategy with which the individual may cultivate a unique style of responses to life's challenges. Through a wide-angled definition I plan to address the fundamental mechanism underlying destructive violence, and through this perspective the spectrum of violence, and ways of approaching it, will be broken down into a more manageable method.

To this end the book is divided into five parts, or realms.

The reader is encouraged to take up his or her birthright to be: *aware, strong, confident, safe* and *happy*. These are the strategic themes I will use to guide the individual to get a handle on the broad topic of aggression.

The first step in self-defence is awareness, particularly of the nature and scope of the problem. Therefore, we will begin by viewing the scope and ramifications of a comprehensive self-defence programme. From here we can begin to tackle the problem from a spectrum of appropriate solutions that range in scale from personal to national.

Before you read any more of this chapter, however, may I suggest that you take a few moments to browse through the rest of the book so as to reassure yourself that your specific and immediate interests will be covered. This chapter highlights the *awareness* aspect of a possible solution to violence. The following chapters offer practical ways to counteract violence. Whichever chapter you choose to focus on, always keep in mind that the views and feelings that you bring to the topic are valuable. So let the contents of this book serve as a springboard to greater self-awareness and expression.

AWARENESS

The following facts and figures are symptoms of a disguised social disease - one that affects each of us in a very personal manner. In order to be effective with self-defence methods, it is necessary to look to the root of this upsetting social problem - violence.

Between the Sexes

Ten years ago the figures stated that one in every four women would be raped. Now this violence has escalated to a new shocking figure, as well as to other areas of society. For example, three out of four wives of the educated middle classes are battered emotionally and physically, and/or raped by their husbands. No longer can the myth continue that violence is the exclusive proclivity of the ignorant and poverty-stricken. It runs through all strata of society. Perhaps even more shocking is the fact that women account for twenty per cent of the physical battering and sexual abuse against children of both genders.

Two nights ago I viewed a faction of violence of even greater societal shock value. It is not enough for those men who mask their weaknesses by perpetrating violence on just those seemingly physically weaker than themselves, i.e. women and children; they have now turned to raping other men.

Cowardice Beyond the Battlefield of the Sexes

No longer is rape singularly the battlefield of men and women. Police apparently find it difficult to come to terms with the existence of male rape. A reporter described the 'uncanny' parallel in the male victim's post-attack re-action. In this particular case, hamstrung by shame, it took the victim two weeks to report his ordeal to the police. He expressed his experience as terrifying and horrendous, one which left him feeling violated and used. He tried washing himself over and over again as though he was trying to wash away the memory that this had actually happened to him.

The report went on to say that the incidence of male rape is on the increase. I wonder if it is the incidence or the reporting of it that is actually on the increase. Most rapes that occur between men are by *heterosexual* men onto other *heterosexual* men. The rapists in this case are seeking even greater levels of dominance and humiliation. The violent act of rape has now made itself known in a universal gender context – one which sheds such an all-encompassing light on the subject of rape that a state of critical mass has been reached. Which way will we go? Do we give up under the sheer weight of this issue as an inherent part of life and succumb to living in fear – wondering if we will be the next victim? Do we badger the police to drop their veil of denial and become more efficient in their efforts to arrest rapists? Do we appeal to the judicial system for more punishing sentences? Do we increase community awareness and action? Do we take the fundamental issue of violence as lacking in our educational systems, and make self-defence available in schools? Do we have laws passed to sanction an increased level of personal weaponry, under the rationale of a need for self-defence?

A chain of ensuing issues threatens our safety on a daily level. Sadly, as is evidenced in the statistics on domestic violence in educated middle-class couples as well as the increased reports of child abuse and incest, many of us have learned to accept the phenomenon of violence as a way of life.

Global Cowardice

There is a haunting litany in the way history repeats itself in the events in eastern Europe. Modern weapons are still used to murder and maim women and children; yet the use of medieval methods to humiliate and demoralize is a staple in the war whose end, ethnic cleansing, justifies the perpetrators' means. This escalating campaign of heinous violence is a daunting cocktail; it shows how history repeats itself even in the face of modern weapons and sophisticated world media exposure and condemnation.

Self-Defence: A Privilege

For the people of the world who are suffering under op-pressive conditions self-defence means survival. And although it should be their natural birthright, the inner strength required for such survival through inhumane, politically-calculated conditions puts people who rely on physical prowess or martial arts alone into a pale light. The whole notion of self-defence classes is a privilege light years away in this context.

Self-Defence: A Right

More and more closet doors open revealing sexual abuse in the childhoods of three out of five adults, increasing spates of violence towards women in open public places, men being raped in the toilets of London's Piccadilly Circus, and men who were neighbours of Croatian men and women now violate them with ease, and with no apparent recollection of their past alliances. What in the world is happening here? We take steps backwards and forwards, all the while side-stepping the heart of the matter. When will we ever learn? The aggressor becomes a complicated creature given the disempowering effects of economic drought and racism. It almost appears that they are driven by these conditions to recover their power by attacking such soft targets as women in wheelchairs, elderly men, mothers taking their babies to the park as a loving act of bonding. And indeed it seems the wealthy are not immune as they frequently become targets themselves.

Each of us has a right to live safe and happy lives. When will the government and criminal justice systems erect and enforce laws that will protect the innocent prey of the cowards? One wonders: is it simply too overwhelming and too late to make lasting changes?

An Open Window for Change

Every structure, every condition is made up of the sum of its parts. Though we may not be able immediately to tackle the world's disasters, we can begin somewhere. One of the most hopeful phenomena of modern awareness is the 'hundredth monkey effect'. This demonstrates how evolution has a resounding and simultaneous effect on creatures across the world. When one of us, whether we be plant, mineral or animal, discovers a better way to do something, the unspoken network of communication is set into motion. There is an echo of an equal nature elsewhere. This effect is also known as morphic resonance, a theory developed by Dr Rupert Sheldrake. For more direct ways of dealing with feelings of helplessness in the face of increasing violence, read *Reclaim Your Power*.

For the remainder of this book I have chosen to build a

strategy for self-defence based on the awareness of the hundredth monkey effect. When we strive to improve ourselves we prime the consciousness of others in other places in the world. Their awakening in their unique cultures and personalities is then felt by us to help fill out our discoveries. The effect is essentially synergistic.

Before laying out methods for combating violence it is important to look at what lies behind the attacker or perpetrator. How does the attacker operate? What motivates their actions and who are the most likely targets?

The rest of this book will be a journey into the inner worlds of each of us for it is in our inner selves that the roots of violence and the solutions begin.

SELF-ESTEEM: THE FOUNDATION OF SELF-DEFENCE

Recently, in an interview about women's confidence and sense of worth I was asked a Pandora's box question by a reporter. She stated something she had discovered about herself and something which also happens to her girl-friends: whenever she had an argument with her boy-friend she went away feeling it was all her fault, as did he. She asked why I thought that happened. I told her she had the choice of a superficial response or the real answer. She chose the 'real answer'. I went on to explain that the answer was an old one, and to be prepared for the sting in the tail of the answer. Remember the garden of Eden story, the storybook version of man and woman? Who was the one who messed up paradise?

'Exactly', I replied.

This interpretation is securely coiled in the back of our awareness as women and is sanctioned by many religions. The degree to which we have left this interpretation unquestioned shows the degree of strength that it wields within the realm of our self-esteem. And if we were so bold and 'arrogant' as to question such bastions of authority, the fear that may discourage our curiosity is that our argument might be dismissed by another theory. A Freudian analysis may say that we have penis envy! This is another old-fashioned idea. It is particularly biased towards the empowered male because it doesn't address something I have found many times over in counselling, i.e. womb envy.

I was delightfully entertained by a woman preacher (one who had been happily married for 50 years, I might add) who in the middle of her sermon delivered her witty version of the Adam and Eve story. She said,

'Well, what's all this talk about women being equal to men? I figured it out a long time ago. God created Adam and said,

"Oh come on, I can do better than that."

Then he made Eve'.

The mixed audience didn't quite know how to respond. With sympathy, I tried to keep my giggling to a mild roar.

SELF-DEFENCE IS NINETY PER CENT MENTAL

As I explained in my first book, *Stand Your Ground*, 90 per cent of self-defence is attitude or conscious use of our mental faculties. Before learning any self-defence strategy we must begin by thinking. When we create space and time in our lives to think, we have more choice. Choice is a crucial step to developing confidence. Having choice in the simple events of our daily lives is what builds confidence.

This is a more process-oriented perspective. When we respect that the macrocosmic goal of self-defence is contained within the microcosmic observations of the moment-by-moment ways in which we are able to release fear, we extend the boundaries of what we feel is possible. Giving ourselves this space and, therefore, time is how and why we become proficient at anything, whether it be dancing, typing, being a parent or brushing our teeth. When we don't feel safe to construct this time and space to meet our needs we become a fertile breeding ground for stress, and put other people's needs above our own. In the extreme situation of an attack, the degree of our love for ourselves, or *self-esteem*, is the crucial motivating factor for fighting back even if that means picking our noses in the face of an attacker.

There are many more subtle ways in which we are attacked in our day-to-day activities. They may involve the way we relate to the many people we love; the stress of coping with challenges and crises; and the abusive voices we allow to breed within our mental and self-doubting emotional selves.

Abuse is the direct opposite of self-esteem. Let's look at the roots of abuse. By shedding light on these often anonymous, destructive forces within and without, we may increase the available energy for self-esteem and self-realization. Through acting on this awareness, this inner light, the choices we make can become even more fulfilling. We may then formulate reserves of strength to break through oppressive situations – in our unique ways – in our own timing.

WHAT MAKES AN ATTACKER?

I feel it is important for us to demystify the two parties in an attack situation. This is of particular importance in the arena of physical violence. Each of us is born with a unique beauty – a unique set of gifts to discover and offer to the world. This unique code is reflected in our individual features. As we move through life our general sense of who we are is shaped by the cultural, environmental and educational systems we encounter in the first twenty years of our lives.

If we are able to appreciate and maintain the balance between the value of our own uniqueness and the rules of social conduct, then we develop healthy self-esteem. People with strong self-esteem are comfortable with both their strengths and limitations. They are able to think clearly. They establish constructive channels through which they may express the spectrum of their emotions.

They find ways to cultivate their physical health via some sort of fitness training and by eating nourishing food. They enjoy learning about themselves in many ways. They are aware of the importance of their image, and enjoy dressing themselves in ways that express their personalities. Overall, a sense of value, directional and moral strength and self-respect (and, therefore, respect for others) are the products of healthy self-esteem.

Take away two or more of these faculties and you will find an eroded self-esteem. This erosion weakens the person's potential to contribute constructively to the community. There is more and more room for the influences of stress, pain, frustration and anger to dominate. When this happens the individual will feel under siege, and as a result, may attempt to compensate and recover this sense of self-worth through other means. The two most convenient categories are aggression and perpetual victim.

Any one of us is capable of becoming an attacker or chronic victim. When one is experiencing a loss of self-esteem, a behavioral pattern develops. This can happen at any age from infancy to adulthood, to those over 60. Generally a lack of the faculties described above is a result of some form of abuse.

SHOCK

When we are abused verbally, mentally, and certainly physically, we go into varying degrees of shock depending on the severity of the abuse and our ability to recover that part of ourselves which may have been temporarily knocked out at the moment of abuse. Some of the signals of being in shock are:

glazed-over look – unable to meet the eyes of others
a blank or continuously dazed look
inability to focus
everything perceived appears grey and one-dimensional
short-temper

a feeling of being disconnected from the ground, feet and legs

All of us encounter shock in minor degrees when something surprises us; this is part of normal living. The body is designed to accommodate a certain level of shock. Sometimes a shocking experience can be the very catalyst we need to jolt us out of stuck patterns. In the Buddhist and Tantric religions, spiritual enlightenment is preceded by an energetic surge of wattage to all of the organic bodily systems, especially the central nervous system. Artists and poets often use their shocking images to herald a new era. Learning about a new culture can be a shocking experience. In these circumstances, when shock is actively utilized to a healthy end, as in the case of expanded awareness, we channel it to aid our personal growth.

However, when shock inhabits our body without productive expression over a period of 21 days or more, we begin to think that its symptoms are a natural part of our nature. This level of shock can remain in our bodies from infancy. The quality of our outlook is blighted; we begin to accept the deadening suppressive effect of this form of pain. But our inner true nature knows better and after a while this truer self begins to detect that something is amiss. At this point we become frustrated and angry. On a subliminal level there is a feeling of imbalance - a mild imperceptible level of pain sets in. We may even develop an injury or other ailment that seems to appear for no reason. When this occurs we either succumb to it and become depressed or we try to gain control of the situation by bullying those in our immediate environments who seem in some way weak. However, because we are not really dealing with the real problem (our own pain and shock), pushing others around does not heal the subliminal pain. So we repeat the action of bullying until it becomes out of proportion with the input we are getting from those we bully. Apart from possible chemical imbalances that lead to aggressive behaviour this is the stuff that motivates an attacker.

To summarize, an attacker was once a victim.

FRUSTRATION AND ABUSE

An Explanation of the Origins of Victim/Attacker Behaviour

Our bodies are a grounded physical boundary (here the word *grounded* refers to the idea of electricity that is safe and channelled). The body keeps what is emotionally appropriate for us, separate from what is appropriate for others. We look and sometimes feel different from others, yet we spend time comparing ourselves to others. When our comparisons result in feelings of inferiority *or* superiority we become unbalanced and lose touch with our individual sense of worth. Whatever the reasons, the loss of self-worth provides the lens through which we approach our daily interactions. An attitude or perspective is created as a result, and we lose the use of our bodies as a grounded physical boundary.

The act of abuse is a response to vulnerability. It is a double-sided coin. On one side of the coin, when loss of self-esteem becomes a ruling motivator in our lives we leave ourselves open to mental, emotional and physical abuse. On the other side we react by abusing others, because any confrontation with our own weaknesses seems unbearable. As a consequence, the abused learns to remain absorbed in his or her weaknesses; the abuser 'acts out' from fear of their weaknesses being discovered. In both cases there is an inherent weakening of character. The whole person, complete with a unique set of interests and responses, is eclipsed by this displaced persona. Confidence breaks down as feelings of vulnerability overwhelm and disintegrate the sense of capability we normally build up from birth.

Ninety-eight per cent of aggressive people were once on the receiving end of mental, emotional or physical abuse, and then went on to use aggressive behaviour to compensate for an inner sense of powerlessness.

Through the Bloodline

This creates an imbalance of force which limits a person's ability to utilize his or her own power in socially constructive and personally fulfilling ways in the world. Children are particularly susceptible, when their immediate environments are sullied by adults in the home and school, who occupy one or both sides of the coin of abuse. The majority of abusive adults were once abused children, and so the bloody cycle persists. For many of us, breaking this inherited cycle of abuse means 'giving up the luxury of being weak'. I see abuse in terms of the bully and the bullied. The bully is an attacker in waiting. This manifests, on the one hand, in the spectrum of abuse we are likely to encounter from others within our lifetimes; but it also often occurs as an insidious omnipresent attacker inside ourselves – a bully/attacker which we may have unwittingly inherited from our parents, and they from theirs. In other words, each of us is capable of being an attacker. Contrary to popular myth, this capability is not exclusive to the mad, sex-crazed stranger who jumps out of the bushes.

A Dislocation from Balance

In the self-defence world the notion of the bully and the bullied, or the attacker and victim, is symbiotic and indicative of a dislocation from the balance of power. That is, they are inter-connected: both the bully and the person who views life from the perspective of a victim have never learned to accept and appropriately express their personal power. Once this lack of expression is exposed, the individual can become capable of bringing about the release of potential self-esteem. The need for self-defence is a direct response to the victim/attacker syndrome.

Healing begins with the recognition of the abuser and the abused inside us. Each of us has had both feelings at some time or another. Perhaps unwittingly the seeds of abuse lie within such actions as, for example, putting ourselves down for no apparent reason: 'Why am I so stupid?', or 'Why am I uglier than everyone else?', and subsequently, feeling the need to put others down in order to feel better about our own problems.

The chronic bully is someone who has learned to suppress any notion of vulnerability or weakness - often as a result of violence inflicted on them. This suppression creates a posture that alienates the bully from his or her more sensitive emotions such as fear, sadness and feelings related to being vulnerable, and, therefore, from a sense of wholeness and balance. Given habitual suppression, this convoluted volcanic emotion can only be released by acting it out on a likely target, that is on one who has taken on the posture of a chronic victim. Instead of developing constructive assertiveness as a solution to the helplessness experienced during vulnerable times, the bully seeks balance outside of him/herself, hence the link to the victim. Energetically, this person's energy field is very spiky; it juts out mainly from the head, chest and jaw.

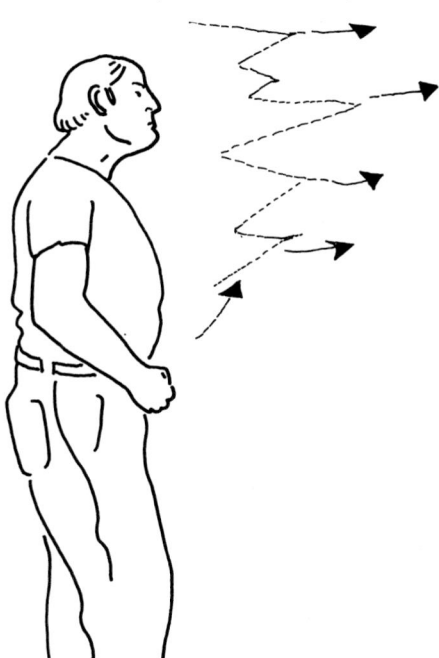

The spiky energy field in this aggressive person is a demonstration of a lack of integrity and confidence.

The vacuum-like energy field of this person is demonstrated in a posture lacking in integrity and shows a depressed self-esteem.

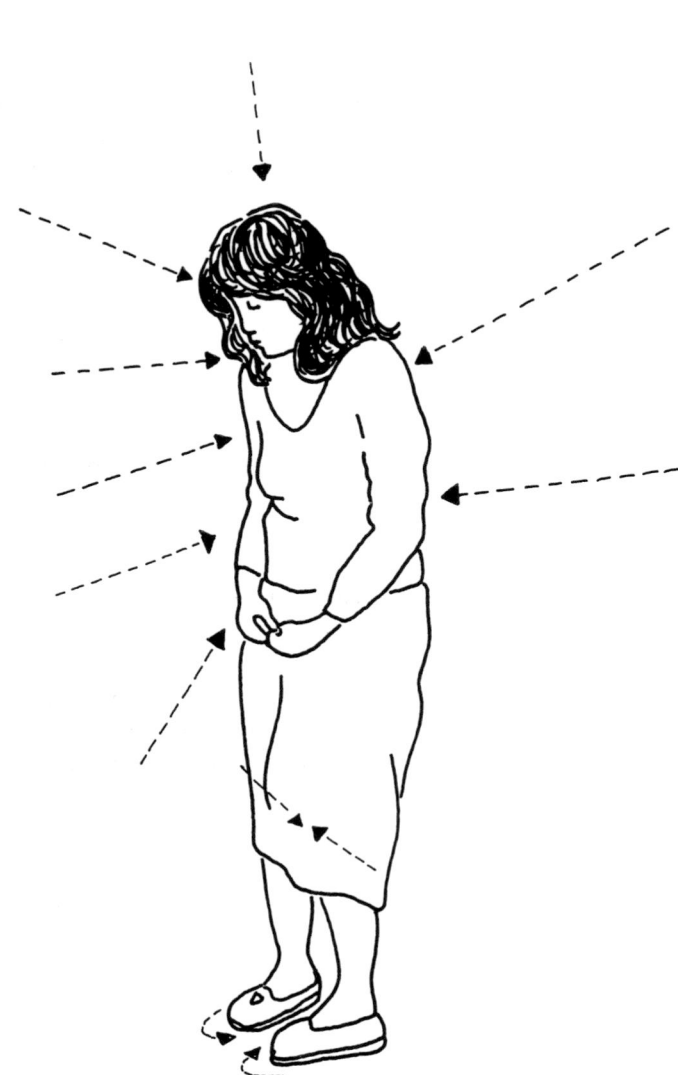

Conversely, the chronic victim is someone who has learned to accept being helpless with regard to others and to life's circumstances and events. A defensive physical, mental and emotional posture develops. Within the shell of this posture the person feels impotent to direct their power outward to effect change within his or her immediate environment. The only apparent survival relief is to implode any feelings of potency, and this especially includes anger. This directs their energy inwards, creating a destructive energy flow which leads to self-abuse.

This energy flow continues to recycle, giving a false sense of balance. On an energetic level it is like a bunch of arrows being sucked into a vacuum, creating a turning-inward effect. This implosion acts as a magnet for any lurking abuser to fulfil his or her fantasy of being less vulnerable and in control by filling the vacuum with their abuse.

Unless this syndrome is recognized there are many moments in each of our days when we could potentially explode into attacker behaviour or revert to impotent victim. There is a body language that is communicated when we are in the role of victim. The language is universal and includes the way we feel when we have been on the receiving end of an aggressive act of racism, classism or other demoralising acts. Sometimes our own internal put-downs breed this body language. What is interesting is that none of us likes to be around someone who is in this posture. The following exercise will allow us to monitor our own responses to the victim posture. I always include this exercise in the beginning stages of self-defence workshops to demystify some of the major reasons for an aggressively-inclined person targeting a person in order to release their frustration with their own impotence.

Exploring the Victim/Attacker Syndrome
You will need a partner for this. Get into the state of mind that says you are worthless. Notice what happens with your head, chest, back, genitals, knees and feet. Now exaggerate this conglomeration of postures. Have your partner follow you as a would-be attacker. They needn't attack you; they simply walk behind or beside you in a menacing way, all the while thinking what they could do to you. Do this for at least one minute.

Mentally note the way you felt while this was happening. Especially be aware of what happened to your sense of time and space. When you feel you have acquired some meaningful information, shake your body as if to shake off the victim posture. Then swap roles, making your partner the victim and yourself the menacing aggressor. Repeat the exercise. Without editing the way you feel toward this person who is cowering in response to your presence, follow them around and without actually doing it, think of what you could do to them. As before, once you have acquired some meaningful revelations stop the exercise and share with your partner what you discovered in both roles, listening for useful information in what they are saying as well.

Though most people acknowledge how uncomfortable and familiar the victim role is they are often surprised to find how aggressive they feel toward the one in victim mode. I have witnessed the most 'proper' ladies' horror when they reported that they 'could have wrung the victim's neck', or 'wanted to hit and knock the person down'. This exercise shows how, given the right circumstances, each of us has the potential to be an attacker.

Honouring Vulnerability as a Useful Tool to Self-Understanding

When we feel vulnerable we can either honour that vulnerability, using it as a means to a better understanding of our most fundamental needs for security, or we may become the victims of this vulnerable state. Being a victim of vulnerability means we are not able to derive any productive meaning from unpleasant experiences. Over time this response becomes a habit and leads to a perpetual state of vulnerability which must find its recourse somewhere. Usually this is in feeling the world and its inhabitants to be one's worst enemies.

Both the aggressor and the victim are attackers. The aggressor expresses this response to abuse outwardly on others. The victim expresses their response to the vulnerability that once led to abuse as aggression against their own potential resources for power. Nothing that may be of beneficial consequence will be considered.

In either case, when we recognize that we have adopted a victim or attacker's posture, we may begin to take steps toward change.

Boredom can Incite Bully-Behaviour

In a recent discussion in my children's class, one of the boys mentioned how we fall into the trap of thinking people who bully are stupid. He went on to state how often those who resort to bullying tactics of a verbal nature are very clever. They know how to say things that are hurtful, and how to escalate the brutal ways in which they say these hurtful things.

This was a very astute observation of his. I will use his observation as a platform for mentioning how frustration that comes from sheer boredom can be a reason why children and adults resort to attacking each other both verbally and physically. Many children are highly intelligent in areas that are not necessarily measured by aptitude tests. The expression of this undervalued talent has to come out somewhere. Usually it comes out through frustration and either leads to aggressive behaviour or, in the case of children who have a more reflective, introverted nature, they can take on a victim posture. This is because they have learned to survive by burying their power, as they have learned to bury their talent.

Untapped Aptitude and Slow Learners

I have worked with several children who have either been categorised as slow learners in school (and who have been tormented by other children for being 'stupid'), or who have come to me to have their bullying tendencies curbed. (Parents often confess that they have bullied the child or that a close relative such as an uncle, aunt or grandparent have bullied the child from birth.)

What I have found in the course of working with these children is that the more complex the movement pattern or concept I introduce them to, the more present and effective they are in carrying out the activity. They rise to the occasion. This has been particularly true of the dyslexic children I've taught. Once they are put into an arena that challenges them mentally or physically, they relax emotionally and are, literally, much happier and radiant, and mentally proficient.

What Can Be Done?

Parents and guardians can minimize aggression and victimization caused by boredom by paying close attention to what (even from infancy) seems to capture a child's interest. Do they respond favourably to music? Or dancing? The things that captivate a child's interest, especially at an early age, should not be ignored. The parent/guardian should do all within their power to illuminate and cultivate these interests.

Guilt — A Disguise for Atonement

A friend recently mentioned that she thought one reason why men seem to be the source of so much of the world's violence and destruction is because they have such a backlog of guilt for atrocities they have committed over history. Rather than acknowledging and transforming this guilt they choose to deal with it by becoming even more aggressive. This is a very interesting point.

The transmutation of abuse is a complicated issue. One should not expect change to happen simply by reading about it. Within the individual the victim-attacker syndrome may be acted out when one feels victimized or embarrassed in any way, for appearing to be vulnerable. This state of imbalance creates discomfort, and once we begin to become aware of it another problem arises - remorse that spirals down into guilt. We must recognize the guilt as a disguise for taking remedial action in order to attain a healthy balance. We can utilize guilt as a signal in the process of healing and as a short term springboard out of the victim-attacker trap, but we should not think of it as a real step out of it. It is a convoluted and debilitating emotion. In fact, it consumes our power to organically transmute the weakness into more balance and inner strength.

Steps Towards Overcoming Guilt

1 Recognize it for what it is. (One of the signals I have come to identify over the years is that dreams of being chased but unable to get away, or if we do move, it is in painful, slow motion, are telling us that guilt is ruling us on a subliminal level.)
2 Break the cycle of beating yourself up mentally and emotionally by doing something nice for yourself. Enjoy it.
3 Do something kind and helpful for someone else, preferably the one(s) you have hurt or bullied.
4 Do your best to come to terms with the reason you feel you have to hurt or bully people as a means for achieving what you want or need.
5 Explore other ways to communicate without hurting others.
6 If you feel you cannot tackle your guilt on your own, seek help from a qualified counsellor.
7 Create a supportive set of friends who will be sympathetic to your wish to change, yet who will remind you when you are backsliding in your journey to grow and be a better person.

OVERVIEW

Self-defence is a very personal topic which begins with awareness of yourself, the reasons why people attack and the cyclical nature of abuse. On the most basic level, awareness of the way in which you communicate with your body can be empowering. Do you live in the body language of a victim or an attacker?

CHECKLIST

☑ **Awareness of Context** Know the dangers of the areas you are getting into (locality and topic).

☑ **Why People Attack** Minimize the attacker's use of the element of surprise against you by knowing why people attack.

☑ **Body Language** Use your body language to minimize the possibility of looking like a victim or a target.

☑ **Guilt** If you have allowed yourself to be an attacker or had the misfortune to be a victim, you may feel guilt. Rather than allow this feeling to take you over, let your guilt be a springboard for change to a healthier, guilt-free person.

☑ **Shock** Beware of the paralysing effects of emotional and physical shock that lead history to repeat itself. See Chapter 4 for self-help first-aid methods to diffuse the disempowering effects of shock.

AFFIRMATION

I am awake to everything I need to be aware of in order to
maintain my sense of well-being.

2 | **The Second Dimension**
THE REALM OF STRENGTH

Having the awareness of the victim/attacker syndrome as the inner foundation and incentive for change is the first step to a fundamental physical and emotional self-defence strategy.

This knowledge affords us the privilege of choice about every response we make to life, whether it is how to deal with personal fears or respond in an aggressive situation, or how to treat the ones we care for. From here we can expand the areas in which we have succeeded as well as build stronger roots for new areas of self-protective action.

Now you are ready to explore the next dimension in self-defence. The awareness you have gained from the key players in a self-defence situation will free up a lot of fear associated with the mysterious attacker.

As you release more energy you may begin to channel it constructively into an outward expression of healthy strength. In the following chapter we will examine the most basic preparation for self-defence: strength.

One can hardly discuss a self-defence strategy without mentioning its fuel. In the light of the previous chapter on what makes an attacker and a victim, and as a prerequisite to this discussion on strength, those who have come through any violent situation with their lives and minds must reframe their description of themselves as 'survivors' rather than victims. Not only will this process of redefining boost one's sense of worth, it will also serve to open up new positive channels for building upon this strength and directing it into other areas that may seem deficient in our lives.

THE POWER TO TRANSFORM

Real transformation can occur when we reclaim the mind/body/emotion connection, and when we realize we may programme this connection to achieve power without it being at the expense of others.

STEP ONE – ANGER CAN BE YOUR FRIEND

Your anger is the warrior of your love and sense of well being. We become angry when our ability to love and be loved is threatened. We also become angry when something disturbs our well being. Dealing with anger is especially difficult for women and children when they have been taught that they have no right to it. Men are usually praised for their ability to get angry and lay down the law. A child may be reprimanded for feeling this natural emotion, especially when this emotion dominates the others. Rather than look at themselves as the source of their children's anger, I have seen parents beat their children because they don't like them to become angry. Perhaps it reminds them of the anger they have not constructively expressed.

A woman is considered difficult or a pushy bitch by members of 'proper' society when she expresses her anger. At best she may be patronized by that classic line, 'Oh, you're so beautiful when you're angry'. **Anger is an emotion that acts as a warrior of the spirit to defend us when we feel our sense of well-being is threatened.** Part of the reason for this is that anger is not encouraged in women as an acceptable emotion to express. What comes up for women on a feeling level is that there is not enough space inside them or in the world to express anger in a constructive manner. We simply have not learned how to make anger work for us. This impoverished space for anger inevitably leads to a feeling that the anger is all-powerful, i.e. if it is expressed it will necessarily be explosive and violent.

How to Accommodate Anger and Vulnerability Healthily

Taking Charge of Your Anger
If you do not feel angry you may need to think of something that makes you angry – perhaps political happenings or women and children being unjustly mistreated. Feel your anger – where is it in your body? Mentally think of your body as a house for an important visitor. In your imagination make this house large and beautiful with solid walls, windows and doors so that you don't feel so threatened by it.

Consider a choice of expressions that may be right for you, such as stomping, yelling, growling. Go to a place where you can feel safe to express your anger in these ways. Notice how regular quality time spent with your anger diminishes the destructive aspects of it and releases more constructive energy for you to pursue the things you were afraid of.

For those who have difficulty in expressing sadness and vulnerability there is an equally impoverished home inside you for this emotion. Apply the same mental exercise as above, making a safe home, large or small, but with soft cushions, watery colours and possibly pools and fountains in the gardens. Alternatively, you may imagine the sea as the home for your feelings of sadness and vulnerability. Mentally go to this place daily until you understand and are comfortable with the productive aspects of your sadness and vulnerability. Make it work for you rather than against you. The act of shutting down your feelings is an internal act of aggression. It will ultimately destroy your sensitivity and you will find yourself acting out this pattern of aggressive suppression on others. Ask yourself: what is on the other side of my vulnerability? What have I learned? If you find you are unable to make this exercise work for you, therapy may be an alternative.

The resilient strength demonstrated in this exercise shows how you can mentally and physically use an aggressive attack to your advantage.

Having someone to talk to can sometimes release pent-up emotion.

Strength: A Personal Matter

When we are called upon to respond to a situation that stretches the boundaries of our normal way of operating, whether it be a new job, relationship, or an uncomfortable degree of violence, we learn about our power, how strong we are.

The traditional view of strength comes in the form of one's physical ability to resist an oncoming force, such as the biceps to biceps attitude in an arm-wrestling contest. In a situation involving physical strength with tightened muscles, then the one who is inherently physically stronger will always have the advantage. Although this is certainly one use of strength, the limitations which surround it as the sole response in a dangerous situation make it a liability in self-defence strategy. This type of attitude to physical strength is conceptually limited and automatically sets up a physical win-lose scenario.

There is another approach, however, which sets up a win-win situation. The attacker's intent is redirected back on to him- or herself, and the one who may have been the victim becomes the director. You may explore this in the aikido 'resilient arm' exercise.

This expression of strength is the foundation for this method of self-defence, as illustrated in *Stand Your Ground*, and sets up an intentional collaboration between mind and body. This is the basis for a whole approach to life and all threatening situations. Power expressed over a period of time (different for each individual) becomes a natural strength. In the above exercise you will find how instrumental your own mental power is in influencing your physical strength. What you did was structure a command, and because the energies of the physical body are largely influenced by our nervous systems, this command travelled from your brain along the impulses of your nervous system to positively or negatively instruct the actions of your musculoskeletal systems. Explore this by giving yourself a negative command such as: 'Oh well they are stronger than I am so they'll probably bend my arm.' Watch what happens to your strength when you influence your physical system in this way. In both cases, when you were strong and when you were weak, it is important to remember that there was something greater than your brain giving the command.

Structure Supports Function

For every successful event such as a social party, a newly constructed house, a piece of music, a film, there is an underlying structure. The structure once existed in somebody's mind. It was then translated into a plan or blueprint, and then the building work took place. Organizing a structure around weak materials weakens its chance for survival. This is why dynamic forms of dance such as ballet and the martial arts place so much emphasis on correctness of stance and form.

If you are feeling weak or particularly vulnerable in some area of your life, it is most likely that the function you are performing is based on a plan that may not have been well organized. All of us have our vulnerable days, but if this vulnerability takes over it is always a symptom of a weakness in our support systems, whether it be home life, family, friends, work or even the structure of our houses and bodies.

Strength as the Ability to Change Your Mind

If you feel any of these potential support systems to be sorely lacking it is time to follow up on your sense of worth and find ways to improve these conditions or to restructure. We can also do this within an instant as was demonstrated in the resilient arm exercise. You simply changed your perception of the person who was trying to bend your arm from being a threat to being a source of power.

In the exercise it was your perception of your strengths and weaknesses which affected your general outlook towards life. You changed your relationship to the situation and to the mental and physical way you were organizing your strength, so consequently, your relationship to the would-be aggressor changed to something much more in your favour. Because this exercise is 90 per cent mental strength at work I have found that people over the age of 60 have a strength that I am not yet able to tap in myself. I can only conclude that their strength is due to their enormous reserves of willpower that have cumulatively enabled them to live through life's challenges. The ramifications of this 'change of mind' and its resulting inner strength are unlimited. It is for you to discover and enjoy. All of the exercises in this book are built upon the use of this inner strength. We will explore this more in the Happiness dimension.

STEP TWO – COMING TO GRIPS WITH YOUR OUTLOOK

If we backtrack for just a moment, in the next exercise you will find how you may use this structuring of command to influence your outlook on any given situation. The value of this exercise lies in building on what already works for you; in other words, building on what is useful. Fifty per cent of your own most effective manner of self-defence is already inside you (one of the major problems with many self-defence courses I have visited is the lack of recognition of the unique styles of the individuals towards the topic). Each individual has his or her own valuable and unique style of self-protection. Each person's style is based on experiences, personality and interests. To this end we will begin with something you may be taking for granted.

Exercise in Perception
You will need a pen and paper.

What is your strongest sense? Seeing, hearing, speaking, touching, tasting or smelling? Perhaps you have more than one. Should this be the case, evaluate which is the stronger of the two.

1 Walk around the room, or in a public area where you feel safe for thirty seconds. Exaggerate your strongest sense to see, hear, smell or touch as many parts of your immediate environment as you can.
2 Write down a summary of what you perceived.
3 Now repeat the exercise. Only this time walk around the same area, and without altering the position of your head, perceive with the idea that your strongest sense is closer to the sky than to the ground. Again, do this for thirty seconds. Then write down a summary of what you perceived this time. Notice any changes from your previous observations. Were you able to see more or less? Was there anything that you noticed this time that proved immediately meaningful to you?
4 Repeat the thirty-second search into your immediate environment with your strongest sense. However, this time, and again without altering the position of your head, walk around as though your sense is closer to the ground than to the sky. Write down your summary of what you noticed this time and note if any of this information was meaningful to you.
5 Repeat the exercise again in the same manner as above, only this time with the idea that your strongest sense lies somewhere between the sky and the ground. Write down a summary of your awareness via this idea.

In which of the levels were you most comfortable? Which level yielded the most useful information?

You may build upon this exercise through various

permutations. For instance, try the same sequence in the same area whilst sitting, lying down or running. You may develop your perception even further by observing the same situation through your thoughts, your feelings and your body. Notice a clearer picture of the same thing when you allow yourself to perceive through all three simultaneously.

The exercise will enable you to use your strongest perceptual sense as a grounding device and will encourage you to be more flexible in your awareness. There may be useful information in our immediate environment that to the untrained person will remain unseen, unheard, etc. Until we are actively using our minds most of us rely upon only one sense to feed back our life experience to us and, as a result, perceive the world and our daily activities through a limited, flat perception. When we use more of the quality focus of our minds we are aware of both detail and overall concepts. This type of perception opens up choice. Choice is empowering. This is an opportunity for you to explore choice whilst in the midst of a challenging situation – one that may require self-defence.

Young children have this innate ability to perceive one situation in many ways, as their imagination, or 'nation of images', has not been so heavily controlled for social approval. The reversal of the teacher-student role is dramatic when I work with children and, of course, the elderly. I present a little information and they tell me in so many ways how this information may be used. As we grow beyond the age of five our imagination is directed toward becoming more 'rational', to the point that as adults, in order to perceive in an open way, we have to retrain ourselves to have this flexible mode of observation.

STEP THREE — BODY LANGUAGE

As mentioned in the First Dimension on awareness, our physical bodies can be used to create a boundary to distinguish our own sense of identity and to make us feel safe and grounded. They keep what is emotionally appropriate for us separate from others. With this in mind we can begin to heighten our awareness of the signals we may be unwittingly giving off to other people. Start by using your expanded outlook from the last exercise to determine which of the levels of perception was most meaningful and empowering to you. When we are in the presence of empowering information we naturally stand taller because truth is ultimately empowering to our nervous systems. Information that is of a life-enhancing nature utilizes the inherent faculty of our minds to make sense of information that appears to be conflicting.

If you discovered that a particular perception allowed you to be more connected with meaningful detail, make sure when you walk, sit or stand, both in public and in private, that you use this to signal that you are at home in your thinking, full of the capacity to feel, and connected to the earth and the sky. With all this in mind you will notice that you are taller without effort, that you breathe more easily and deeply, that your body feels lighter, and that you have the feeling of existing within a protective, radiant, invisible sphere. Explore three different ways of expressing your self-esteem through your body:

1 withdrawn, empty and depressed
2 overly puffed up, arrogant, excessive
3 feeling the balance between being full of power, yet relaxed and naturally radiant

Fitness: A Source of Strength

As we look at strength it is important not to omit an obvious source of strength: fitness. Keeping our bodies as fit as possible through walking, swimming or sport only reinforces all that we have learned about strength so far. Hatha and Iyengar yoga, Tai Chi, Kung Fu and Chi-Kung build strength, flexibility, resiliency and peace of mind. Gymnastics and dance are excellent forms of fitness and are especially suited for children.

When we know what our bodies are capable of doing we compound our level of self-esteem. Stamina, muscular strength, coordination, balance, a sense of timing come from keeping our bodies on the pulse of fitness. We also have an edge in meeting challenging situations because stress is kept in check through exercise, and so are our reflexes. If you are serious about developing and maintaining a self-defence strategy make sure to include cardio-vascular activity and stretching as staples to your programme of training. Three times a week is usually an adequate minimum, though if you have doubts, be sure to consult your physician first. Below you will find a simple exercise routine that efficiently gets the blood and oxygen pumping into all the muscles of the body and, equally, sharpens our mental acumen.

Recovering the Physical Boundary: The Six Empowering Exercises

These exercises are used as a warm-up for Kung Fu. They will take about five minutes at the most once you have learned them. They provide a good warm-up for self-defence training and just about any sport as well. They may also be done each morning as a way to keep you fit for the challenges of the day:

1 Hip Circles
With hands on your hips and feet together, circle your hips nine times both directions. I call this Around the World when I am working with children.

2 Knee circles with extension – skier's exercise

Keep your feet together. Place your hands on your knees. Circle them around, pushing them into an extended position when they reach the back part of the circle. The combined action of circling and extending makes you go up and down. This is a good aerobic exercise. I refer to it as the 'pogo stick' for children. Do this nine times before switching to nine repetitions the other way.

3 Long stretch

This is also known as 'monkey stretch'. This exercise stretches all the long muscles of the body, and especially focuses on the entire back, arms and legs.

Stand with feet together or apart, parallel under your shoulders. Interlace your fingers together and, keeping your legs straight, stretch down toward your feet. Then stand up again with your interlaced hands above your head. Next, turn your upper body so that it twists gradually to the side, and bend down to the side. Stand up and repeat on the other side.

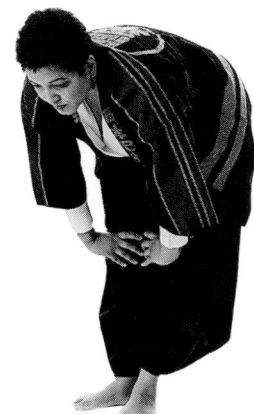

4 Hamstring Stretch

Shift your weight so that 70 per cent is on one leg. Extend the other leg and rest on your heel at a 45 degree angle to the direction you are facing, keeping the weight in the back leg. Interlace your fingers again. This time extend your hands and chin down toward the foot that is resting on its heel. Be sure to keep the majority of your weight in the back leg. Keep extending your chin and interlaced hands down toward the toes that are up. You will feel a stretch in the back of the leg that is extended and in your lower back. Do not jerk or bounce during the course of this exercise. Keep to an elliptical motion. Do this nine times and then repeat on the other side.

5 Bow and Arrow Tiger Claw Diagonal Stretch

This exercise warms you up to the wide-horse stance used in Kung Fu and Karate. It also stretches all the muscles located on the front and back diagonal lines of your body from hip to opposite shoulder.

Stand with your feet wider than shoulder width. Make one hand into a claw. Reach across in a half-circle to your opposite foot, stretching the muscles that run diagonally in your back. Using the claw hand, grip tighter with the top joints of your fingers, shift your weight to 70 per cent on the back leg, and at the same time draw your elbow up and back diagonally, to a position above your head. This motion will expand your chest muscles, strengthen your legs, stamina and your ability to breathe a bit better. Continue to go from side to side repeating these motions a total of nine on each side.

6 Bucket Swing

This exercise strengthens the lungs and diaphragm. It also loosens the shoulders, increases circulation to the hands, legs and feet.

Assume the wide-horse stance as in the previous exercise. Turn your torso sideways into a near perpendicular relation to your legs. Swing your inside arm backwards for only nine revolutions. As you get to nine bring up the other arm so that they swing together above your head, parallel to each other. Now let both of them drop to the top and middle of your other thigh. Then turn to face the other side and begin swinging the new inside arm back as before up to nine counts and continue to repeat this five times on each alternate side.

Note: Once this level of repetitions becomes easy you may increase the number to twelve repetitions for exercises 1–5, and eight on the bucket swing exercise. You may also increase the speed.

Basic Ways of Moving in a Strong Way

Before you think about moving your body in self-protective mode you must be aware of your basic steps. Think of yourself being pulled by the arm. You can express your strength by standing your ground and pulling away from the aggressor or you can move in the direction of their pull as in judo and aikido. In your mental rehearsal, notice what your feet are doing as you move toward the aggressor. Are they crossing over each other to fill the distance? If so, you must rewind your mental rehearsal tape and start again because crossing your feet will only trip you up and defeat your purpose (see Figure 1).

Figure 1 The crossed feet show how one can potentially trip oneself up in an attempt to escape.

Move in a parallel manner as in Figure 2. This way of moving keeps your body in an open alignment so that you may sense the intent of the aggressor and move more efficiently. You may also move in the fencer's mode as demonstrated in Figure 3.

Figure 2 The parallel move.

Figure 3 The balance of the figure on the left is potentially stronger than that of the aggressor on the right.

Strength as the Ability to Remain Still

One of our problems as women is that we focus on what isn't working by wishing and hoping: 'If only I were more beautiful; if only I were wealthier', etc, etc. This masquerades as wanting to improve ourselves though it really only serves to put us down. When we take inventory of what we do have versus what we don't have we build a positive base from which to expand. Keeping quiet and accepting stillness as a form of strength may be just what we need when we encounter stressful situations.

> When there is stillness in the motion of our days, life's mysteries are revealed.
> CHINESE ADAGE

A few moments of quiet afford us a sense of inner space. Where there is more space there is more time. Where there is more time there is more choice. Where there is more choice there is more of a chance to achieve our intentions. There are many forms of meditation that one can take up. A good start is by practising a very simple exercise:

Sit or lie down on your back with your feet up on a suitable chair at home or on your break at work. You can begin with 5 minutes once a day and then increase the frequency of your relaxing time as much as you like. Try to clear your mind. Sometimes focusing on a pastel sheet of colour can help you. If, however, you find that the thoughts will not leave your head use your mental power to make them expand to get even bigger and louder until finally exhausted, they will be happy to leave the home of your mind.

You will find many benefits in doing this. For one, your emotional fuse will seem a lot longer. You will have a clean slate upon which to develop your thoughts or to learn something new, and you will find yourself remaining happily detached from situations that normally get on your nerves. This is because we free more energy when we are still. When we have more energy we can be a little more magnanimous with our time. Also, a moment of reflection may give you what you need in the apparent fast action of an aggressive situation. Our instincts and intuition reside within the still places inside us. Fear and frustration keep us from appreciating the stillness.

SUMMARY OF STRENGTH

Here is an example from one of my pupils that summarizes a use of the strength dimension. She is fifteen years old, a relatively happy-go-lucky individual at this dramatically changing stage in her life. She had successfully dealt with the traumatic adjustment required in changing schools and well as with the trauma of transforming her relationship with someone who had bullied her severely into a blossoming friendship. The only thing that really bothered her was the continuous threatening atmosphere emitted by some of the ever-present bullying cliques at school. This bothered her so much that sometimes she found herself getting depressed after meeting them on a daily basis.

She had already brilliantly analyzed their reason for needing to be in cliques in the first place at an earlier session; she had observed some of the members of the cliques on their own, to find that each of them on their own treads upon shaky ground. The puffed-up, confident bully seemed to wane into a shrivelled introvert. I acknowledged how accurate her observations were and how much more naturally confident she was to be able to have this perspective, though somehow with school just around the corner her trepidation regarding this aspect of her impending social environment seemed the most pertinent of her concerns. This established the day's lesson.

First of all I asked her to say more about her social scene: How many cliques of bullies were there usually? Who were her allies? How many groups of friends did she have? Who were her beacons of inspiration? She acknowledged an abundant selection of friends as well as the possibility to reach out to one of her teachers and counsellors if the need arose. This acknowledgement brought a lengthening of her posture and a bit more light in her eyes. With this information I set about illustrating in my crude way a sample social-environmental map.

After receiving confirmation about the relative accuracy of the crude map I asked her to illustrate her general movements through the setting. She did. Next I asked her to reflect upon a time when she had successfully defused the aggressive atmosphere of the threatening group. What had she done?

I was very impressed with both her nonchalant, yet masterful strategy and the natural ease with which she so swiftly executed her strategy. What she described, however, piqued my interest even more. She had been walking by a clique as usual when she saw one girl being insulted and physically threatened by them. She just happened to approach the scene from behind the bullies. As she drew near she couldn't bear what she saw happening yet again.

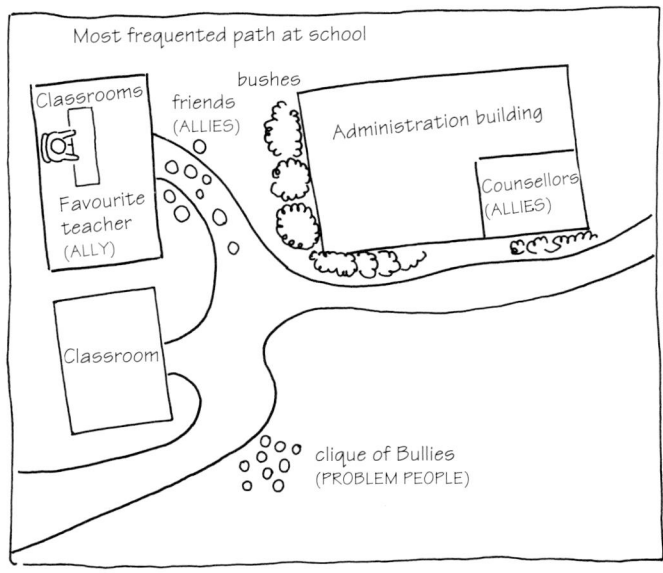

Heroine's social-environmental map.

She said that in what felt like a flash of the moment, she reviewed all the things that she could do (going to the aid of the girl in trouble or shouting at the bullies). This moment disappeared and she found herself as though moved by something 'not her', something even possibly outside herself, gently guiding her to stay on the side of the bullies. For a moment it looked as though she had abandoned her amiable nature to join the bad guys. Instead she used her physical presence to gain their trust and then asked them what they were doing. How could all of them possibly be offended to such an extent by one single and much smaller new girl? It was as though she had thrown the misguided pack of dogs a bone to chew. They immediately retracted their abusive attention from the stunned new girl and began talking amongst themselves about why they were offended by the shoes she was wearing. At this moment the young heroine walked away with the girl, leaving the pack arguing over who was most offended and why.

Below is a sequence that maps out the heroine's

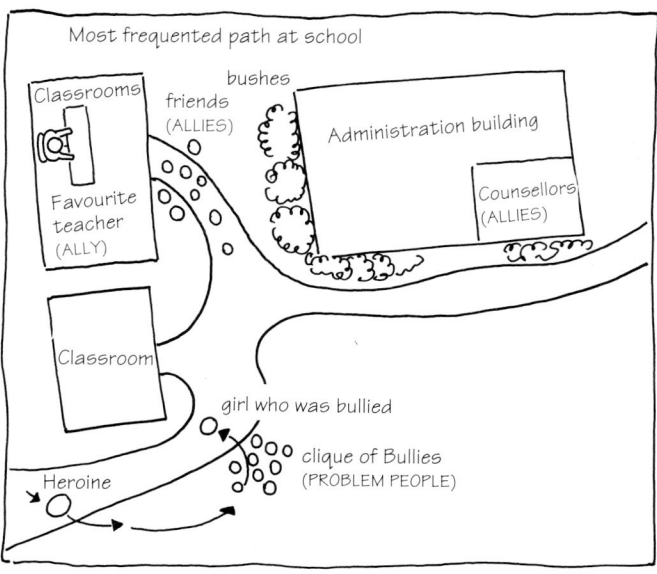

Path of the heroine's movements.

movements that led to success in her threatening social environment.

The heroine in this situation was strong in that she stayed in touch with her anger toward the bullies. In her moment of stillness she translated that anger into constructive action that had an educational impact on the bullies. She was agile in her approach when she did the unexpected by removing the conflict of the bullies' potential aggressive action towards her, by first looking at the situation from their perspective. She used her voice in such a successful way because she was able to hear the bullies' point of view. Essentially, she naturally put into practice a high-level Kung Fu concept which is used for developing strength: she conquered the tiger by becoming the tiger.

OVERVIEW

Strength is what you have inside you to maintain your sense of well-being and the way that you protect all that is valuable to you.

Remember that anything that you have survived can be a reliable source of strength. Also, awareness and acceptance of your strengths *and* your vulnerable areas will build inner strength. This flexible inner strength will give you more mobility to achieve your goals, whether they be life goals or dealing with a threatening physical situation.

CHECKLIST

☑ **Uniqueness** When we accept and stand behind our uniqueness we become strong and fuel ourselves from within.

☑ **Change and Grow** The ability to change from a frustrating habit to a healthy constructive way of achieving your goals is a demonstration of strength.

☑ **Survivor** Relabel areas of your life in which you have felt a 'victim' to 'survivor'. Feel the strength that you have as a result of being a survivor.

☑ **Anger and Fear** Use anger and fear as sources of strength. Make them work for you rather than against you.

☑ **Resilient Strength** If you find yourself using the arm wrestling type of strength and you are getting nowhere, remember the resilient arm type of strength and use it mentally and physically.

☑ **Structure and Function** Remember structure supports function. If you are not succeeding in some area, check the organization. Reorganize the way you are using your body, and the plan you have set into motion.

☑ **Fitness and Confidence** Confidence is the product of strength. Keeping fit is one of the best ways to increase your confidence and to keep up your levels of physical/emotional security. Find a way to keep fit that you enjoy. Fitness (when used in combination with awareness) produces a strong, radiant, non-victim-looking person.

The six empowering exercises which are explained in this chapter are an excellent way to begin your daily fitness regime. They only take five minutes, too.

AFFIRMATION

I learn from all difficult situations. I turn aggressive opposition to my advantage.

3 | **The Third Dimension**

THE REALM OF BEING CONFIDENT

When our sense of self-esteem is intact we become focused and confident. Being confident is the product of being able to be still and accepting of both strengths and weaknesses. When we are in a confident state we can more clearly discriminate between our own intentions and those of others. All of us have experienced this state of confidence at some point in our life; for some it has been a more fleeting experience than for others. In this chapter we will work to cultivate and maintain the state of being confident in the way we think, feel, move and, generally, in the ways we express ourselves.

CONFIDENT MOTION

Out of self-esteem and the strength that surrounds stillness comes an effective way of moving. As we discussed in the last chapter, structure supports function. Now we will work with ways to evade aggressive attempts by attackers, who I will now refer to as cowards, to restrain us. To start with we will review the use of the mind/body connection. When our intent is strong enough the commands our minds give to our bodies can immediately strengthen or weaken the body. This communication loop will be interrupted if there is vertebral misalignment, ligament damage or organ damage. We may feel that we are blocked up in certain areas to the point where there is little or no movement. Obviously, this lack of mobility can be the result of diseases such as multiple sclerosis and paralysis (though in these cases, once the disease has established itself in the body and one learns to move in other ways, it is possible for the mind to strengthen the entire system so that those who have been challenged in these ways can maximize their strengths. And certainly the inner strength required to overcome these challenges will be even greater in these cases).

Later we will see how influences on the body eventually shape the mind. The mind/body connection is set up so that a challenge to either side affects the other. In other words, just as our mental strength becomes reflected in our physical side, as in the resilient arm exercise, the way we move in our bodies affects the way we think. This process of the body affecting the mind is much slower than the other way around. The mind gives a command to the body and it is immediately received. The body, on the other hand, stores all of these commands and takes on an atmosphere which, over time, will house the mind and affect our outlook to the point of influencing the future commands of our minds!

In the ancient healing martial art, Chi-Kung, 'the way we move is the way we live'. So it follows that if we practise movements that are stiff and angular our thinking eventually takes on these qualities. However, if we move in fluid, extended ways, our mental faculty to plan ahead and to move gracefully through life's transitions is reinforced. With this in mind we will begin the notion of being confident through ways of moving. The success of all the physical self-defence techniques will be based upon confident movement.

Confident Movements: Advance and Retreat
In a physical self-defence situation, movements toward or away from an aggressor form the base of what we do next. The art of fencing is the art of offence and defence. As spectators we watch as the fencers advance and retreat from each other. The reason they do this is to extend or close time. Space equals time. When we have little space our sense of time is limited. So the fencers exploit this

Body impacts mind.　　　Mind impacts body.

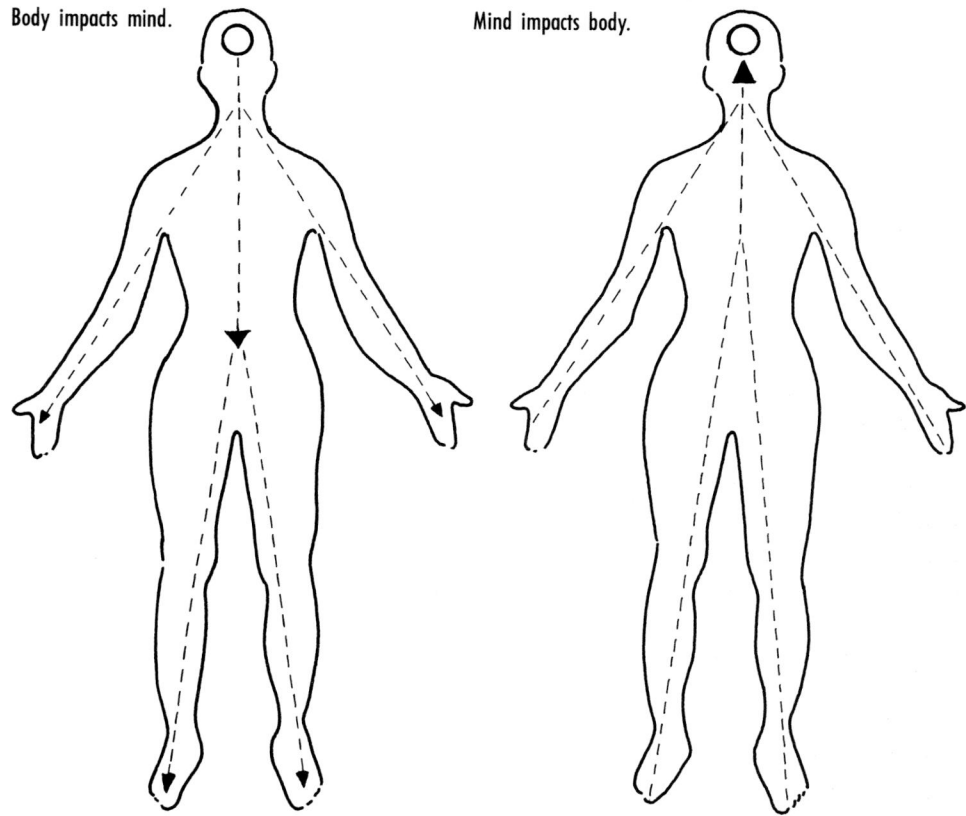

knowledge by using their bodies to create space for themselves either by actively retreating or by asserting themselves by advancing to 'take ground' away from their opponent.

You may incorporate the use of this information into a confident way of moving toward and away from a cowardly aggressor. This way of moving may be familiar to you from partner dancing where one person follows the other.

1 Prepare yourself by mentally organizing your body as though it were suspended from the heavens by a delicate

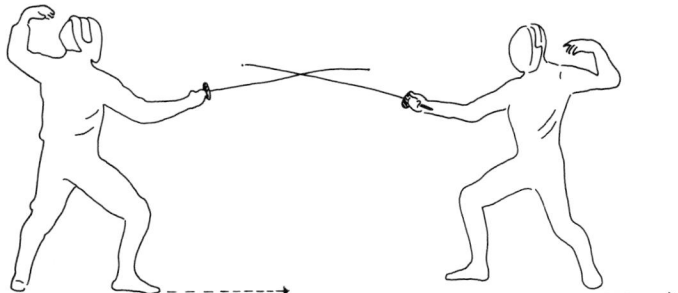

By moving in a unified manner the fencers create space and time in which they may initiate offensive or defensive plans.

yet strong silver cord which runs down through your spine into your legs and down to your feet. Your connection to the earth is through an almost electric tingling feeling in your feet. Over time this will give a lot of energy to your roots, your legs and feet. Feel the stillness inside you.

2   Out of the stillness move forward three steps and then retreat three steps in the manner shown opposite.

Be sure that your arms move with you rather than

letting them swing out of control. Also, be aware that you are keeping the sense of stillness inside as you move.

3 Now move to the side in a sliding motion three steps to the left and then three to the right.

4 Advance and retreat diagonally three times. Do this on both legs.

5 Once you feel comfortable with moving in these ways whilst maintaining your inner stillness, vary the numbers by increasing the amount of advancing movements and minimizing the retreats. An unlimited number of combinations are possible.

6 Now repeat steps 1-5 with an imaginary person moving toward you.

7 After you feel confident in this exercise on your own, bring in helpers. Tell them to try to grab or push you in various ways so that you may rehearse moving out of harm's way.

She takes her first step in escaping the cowardly mob by moving decisively with the flow of their aggressive pushes and pulls. Alternatively, you may take quick, confident walking steps.

8 Once you have become proficient at moving in this way, move into action so as to intercept the aggressive coward's intent to harm you before they move. You've heard the phrase, 'Don't you even think about doing that!' This is the mental perception that goes with your body's perception as you almost read the mind of someone who wishes you ill.

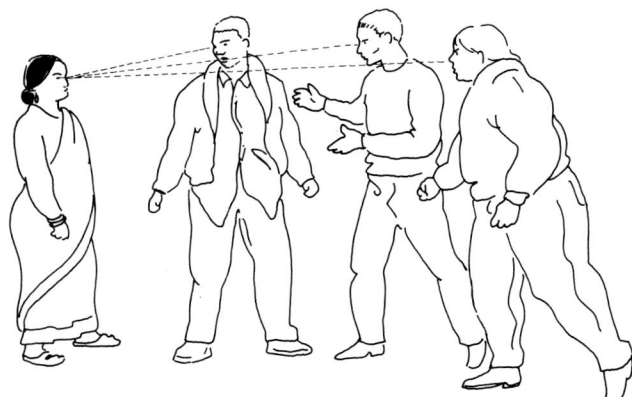

Though seemingly difficult, making eye contact with the cowards can be empowering, especially when she looks directly at the leader of the mob.

Using your body as a radar system, as you do when you move in the above way, will sharpen your mind to detect the intent of an aggressive coward. You will find that as you improve in this area of detection you can sense danger across the road and increasingly move away before it becomes a physical confrontation.

Moving Through Crowds: Dragon Walking
In large, densely-populated cities we may find our ability to get to our destinations impeded by many people who are mindlessly walking about without a sense of purpose. This can be very frustrating, but you may use this situation to sharpen your ability to find an opening where there appears to be none.

In the East the dragon is a symbol of celestial power and freedom. It moves freely through the clouds, and if ever it encounters any obstacles, it is able to change its shape to become any size or thing it wishes.

This exercise is a fun group game and a tool for rehearsing moving through rush hour crowds. It also sharpens your ability to lead and to increase your sensitivity to others when you are in such a position.

You will need at least eight people for this.

1 Form a line with you as the leader. Instruct the others to follow the person in front, maintaining arms-length distance for the entire exercise. Then start walking straight forward until everyone is comfortable following. As you do it encourage everyone to walk as though comfortably suspended between heaven and earth. Keep the inner stillness whilst in motion throughout the exercise. Keep your chest and throat open and move smoothly as though you are walking on clouds.

2 Now turn and move toward the group so that you are about to form a circle, only don't wait for the last person. This will give you the opportunity to find an opening between people to cut through with your body/mind. Everyone will then follow this weaving motion.

3 Next, lead your group through twists and turns as though you were describing the shape of a dragon's tail. Take them into a circle that runs anti-clockwise and then finish by taking them into a clockwise circle. You will be several steps ahead of the 'dragon's tail', so while they are just about to complete the anti-clockwise motion, change your direction to clockwise. Judge the time and distance it will take for everyone to finish so that you finish in a smooth and almost magical circle.

The Element of Surprise

When we are confident, our sense of timing can work wonders for us. We can defuse potentially distressing situations by dealing with the source of the problem, rather than defusing our own power by responding to the symptoms. In the following examples the individuals are confident in their awareness as they are able to use spontaneously the element of surprise. The setting was a world congress meeting with doctors, scientists, politicians and some martial artists. A friend and colleague of mine was socialising when one of the scientists, referring back to the way I had been introduced, said in a quarrelsome tone,

'How can *she* be a master? She is a woman!'

To which my friend quickly retorted, 'Well, they don't take well to being called mistresses!'

Submissively, he replied, 'Oh, of course not. Yes, yes, I see.'

We have all seen examples of people responding, often with courage, and because they remained confident in the face of other people's intentions.

I recently heard that the actor Michael York was almost attacked by a gang of men while he and his wife were walking on a beach in Brazil. The gang approached them

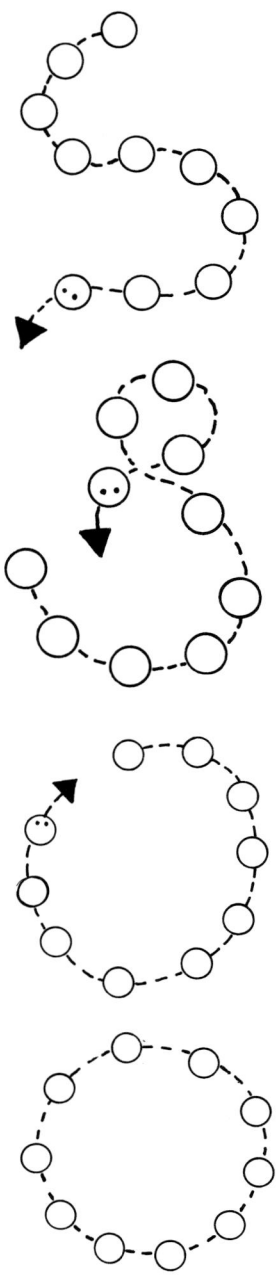

Opposite: Dragon walking will improve your mental and physical agility to make quick decisions, such as finding an efficient way through a crowded street or coping with daily pressures.

with broken bottles and knives. Michael moved through his terror and drew upon a resource from his acting tools, his voice. He let out a very loud sound and drove the cowards away.

Out of awareness, our potential to centre is heightened by the knowledge that bullies are really weak cowards, who have learned a little aggression to mask their insecurities. This mental awareness can send a signal to our fear reflex in an aggressive situation and mentally reduce the attacker to a mass of weak jelly. Having the knowledge of the physical vulnerabilities of a person who is not treating you with respect can free up time for you to sense the real intent of an attacker.

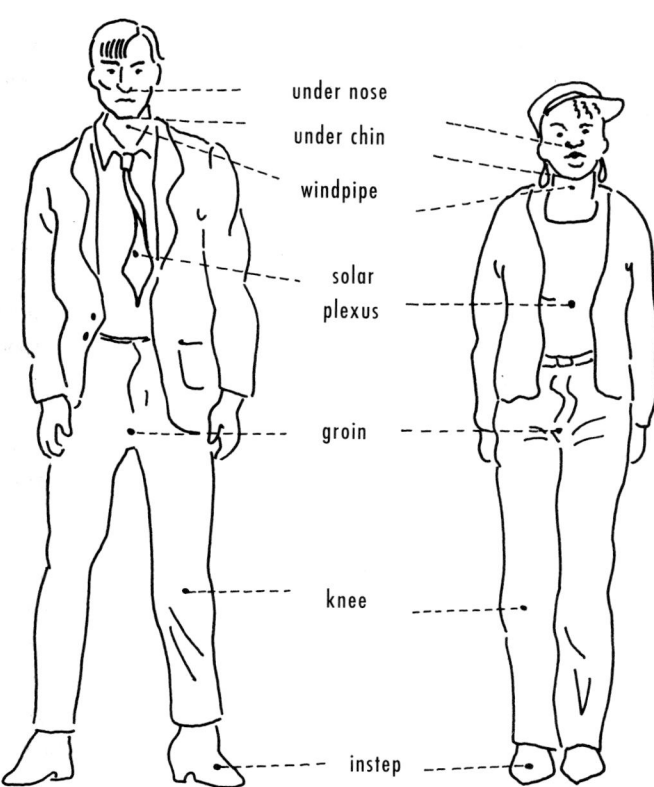

under nose
under chin
windpipe
solar plexus
groin
knee
instep

Vulnerable points.

Some women have realized at knife point that their attackers were really afraid and when they mentioned their realization verbally they dropped their weapons and burst into tears. This may not always be the case. The coward's deeply-seated insecurity may not be so visible and you may have to respond in another way.

WING TSUN

A Chinese woman, Wing Tsun (also spelt Wing Chun), whose name means 'beautiful spring', developed a martial art form that was to revolutionize shaolin kung fu. This is one of the major systems that Bruce Lee used to develop his famous skills which he called Jeet Kun Do.

The story begins with Wing Tsun as a petite, beautiful woman who lived with her elderly father. Admiring her beauty, one of the local bullies decided he wanted her for his own. He demanded to marry her when he returned from his travels. Wing Tsun and her father wanted no part of this unsavoury character, so her father suggested that she go to one of the monasteries to learn martial arts from one of the skilled nuns named Ning Mui. She studied for a short time and returned with her extraction of *silum tao* or 'the little idea'.

When the bully returned to claim what he thought was his chattel, she said she would fight him in front of the community members. If she lost she would concede to marry him. He laughed in disbelief. After a while she managed to convince him that she was serious so he confidently said he would humour her foolish folly. Mockingly, he threw one punch at her which she deflected . . . then another, with the same result . . . another . . . and when he became angry and really went for her with full force, not only did she deflect his punch, she redirected his power back onto him and somehow knocked him flat out with her deflection.

This was hitherto unheard of in the martial arts world. Usually in a deep stance you deflect with one arm and retaliate with the other. She had managed to do both with one arm, and at close range, with the other arm held back in reserve. The marriage was off and Wing Tsun went on to teach a select group of high-level martial artists her technique.

What is revolutionary about Wing Tsun is the concept which is reflected in the stance, and the defensive/offensive aspects of the art. Instead of the wide-low stance, she adopts a stance which accommodates and uses a combination of the fear and panic we may feel when attacked, and the cool, calm, collected perspective we have when viewing something from above. She uses the 'goat-riding stance' to create a triangular base. This base is stable for fluid movements and the funnel shape created by the feet is the base for the beauty of her technique: the efficiency of the direct route between two straight lines. Here is a prime example of how strategic structure allows for efficiency in function. The stance allows for maximum release of force with minimum effort. It is also designed for maximum close-range defence. A third element comes into play when the practitioner masters the offence/defence tactic: the ability to *use your arms as radar* to sense the intent of the other person split seconds before their intent enters their arms to attack you. This is an advanced level of Wing Tsun; one that, given skilled instruction, can be achieved fairly soon. At this level Wing Tsun taught that you can 'borrow power' from the cowardly attacker. This is similar to the awareness in maximizing your strength which you gained in the resilient arm exercise in Chapter 2. We will now explore some of the essential ingredients of the Wing Tsun system.

The Wing Tsun Weapon

Wing Tsun believed that too much time is wasted in movements that are not direct, such as the brawling round house swing.

So her striking technique is set up to be direct.

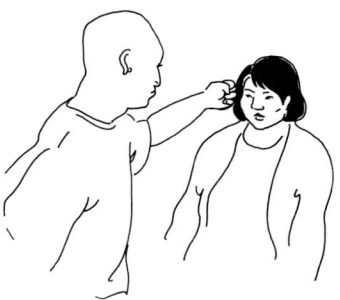

Striking through the target.

Again, you will see that the contracted position describes the inner contraction we may feel when we are afraid or in brief moments of panic. However, the structure doesn't stop here. The stance may look weak but it is not. It effectively exaggerates then transforms the 'emotional content' into fuel for power, but then brings it out into a powerful plus. In the punching set-up the fists are coiled back like a strong spring. One fist is extended (using the unbendable arm feeling) whilst the other one is held in reserve as a back up. The arm held back may also remain open to double as a defensive move. This set-up allows the punches to move as though they are being sucked into the tunnel of the other person's strategic target area, the nose.

Effective strategy for chain punching.

Chain Punching for Stamina and Circuit Building
A continuous flow of reserve is created in the chain punch.

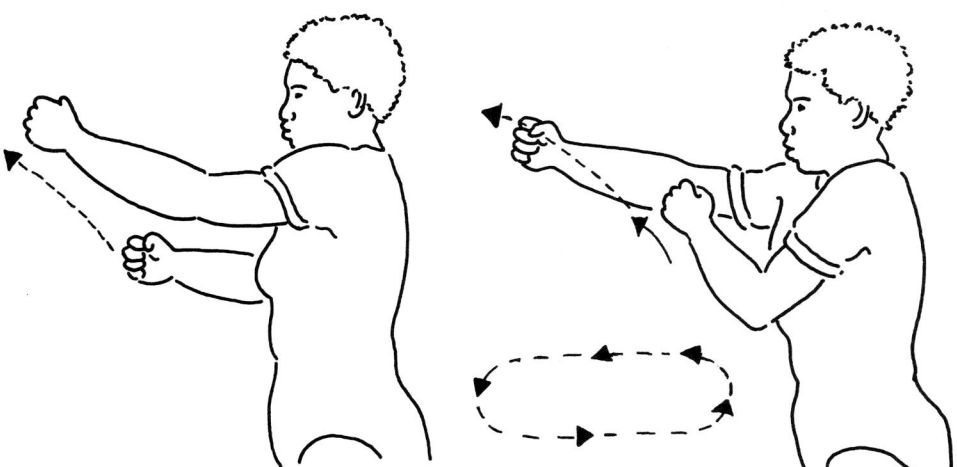

The chain punching exercise develops two important self-defence faculties:

1 It builds a strategic stamina that may be required in a physical confrontation.
2 It allows you to build up a circuit of force.

This circuit becomes magnetic to the point that you may use it as a radar to upgrade your speed reflex in order to detect your opponent's next move. Practise this daily for one minute during the first week. Be sure to practise with an imaginary or real target in mind, otherwise your training will have no meaning, and will be wasted. Once you can train with full mind and accuracy for one minute then increase your time gradually to fifteen minutes.

Wing Tsun's martial arts sophistication is exemplified in her awareness that the thinking mind is at the root of a coward's attack, so why waste time aiming for the stomach, neck or chest. An accurately-directed strike to the nose causes varying degrees of shock to the brain. This immediately stops the coward from attacking by redirecting their attention back on to themselves rather than you. After all, their thinking mind is the commander of their actions. In fact, by directing your strike through the nose target you will be striking at the entire centre line of the other person. The centre line includes the spine and central nervous system.

Dealing with Close Range Attacks

The Wing Tsun technique comes into its own at close range in the lift/elevator, the limited space of a car, or when one is backed into a corner. It exemplifies the balance between yin and yang, in that you may use your arms in a receptive mode to detect the aggressive coward's next move while your arms are extended in the yang on-guard position.

Whilst keeping distance is a valuable self-defence strategy, the Wing Tsun technique allows you to move in close to the coward, especially within their arm's reach, and this can be to your advantage.

This idea of moving into an almost intimate position with your aggressor is particularly useful when their arms are longer than yours. Besides being a revolutionary concept in self-defence, it is a clear example of the *element of surprise*.

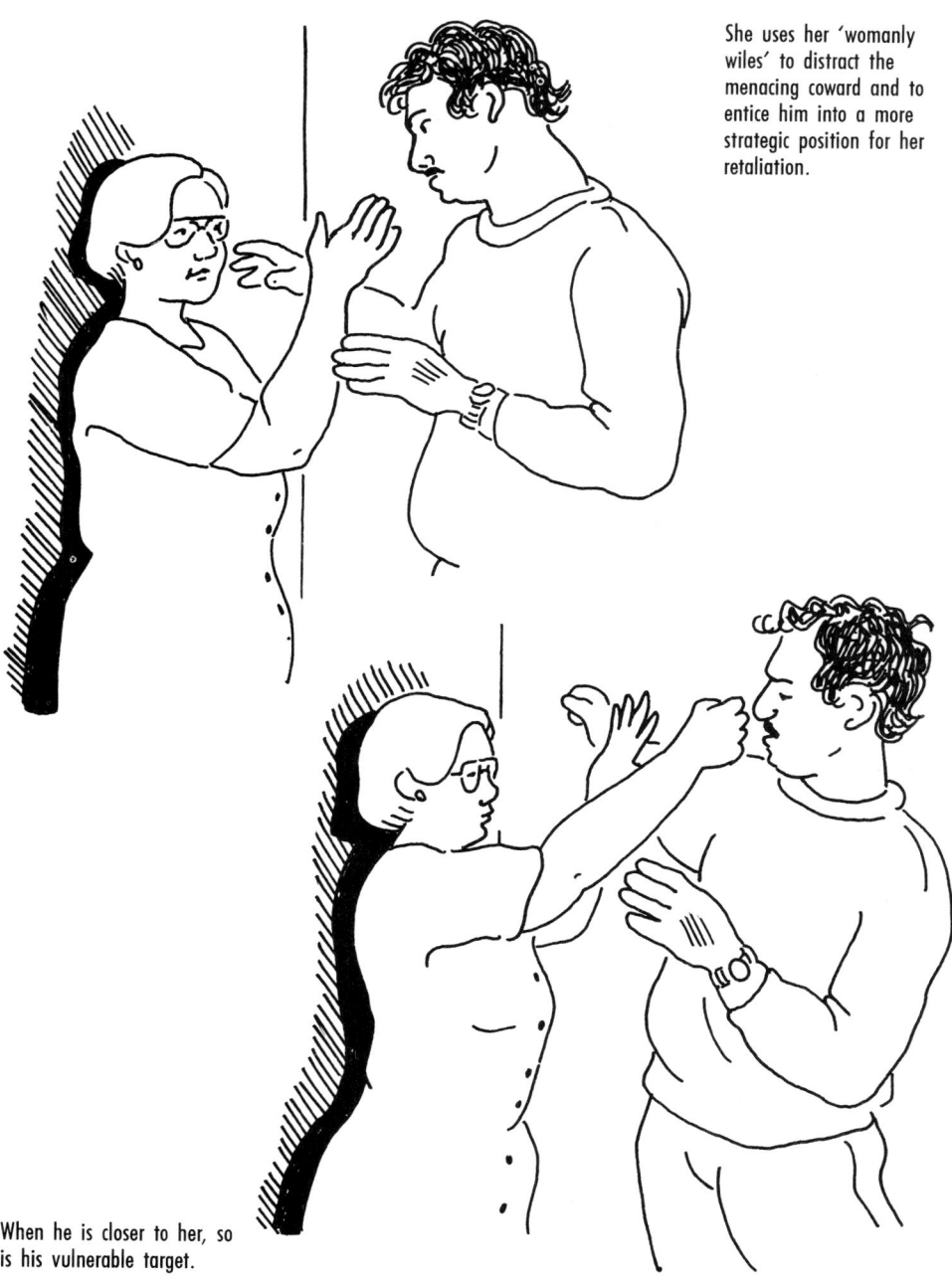

She uses her 'womanly wiles' to distract the menacing coward and to entice him into a more strategic position for her retaliation.

When he is closer to her, so is his vulnerable target.

The Vulnerable Rectangle: Strategic Targeting

Wing Tsun's 'little idea' says that the major vulnerable
parts of our body are in the rectangular box which begins
at the top of the head and ends just below the groin. This
is a highly strategic map. It concentrates on the most
vulnerable parts of the body, both for purposes of
protecting yourself in case someone strikes out at you, *and*
for retaliation. Before getting into the technique you might
explore waving your arms around alternately in front of
this box of your vulnerable areas. Be sure to keep the
extended feeling you had in the resilient arm exercise as
you play with your natural reflexes.

**It is good to take care of this area of self-defence early
on, as no matter what other techniques one learns,
the fear of what to do if someone hits at you can drain
confidence in other skills you may have acquired.**

The On-Guard Position
You will need a partner for this. Alternatively, imagine
someone who is bigger and/or stronger than you.

This defensive technique is very similar to the post
or extended foil position in fencing. I find it to be
immediately accessible, especially when I use it in
teaching children to defend themselves. The key to this
technique is to not get stuck in any of your responses, not
to be attached to how well you deflected one punch,
because all of your attention will go into this gloating and
your reflexes will not be sharp to deal with another punch
that may be right around the corner.

1 Stand with the large toes of your feet facing each other
so that your feet form a triangle. Press out from your
outer thighs as though your knees were loosely tied
together with rope. This may feel a bit strange as your
feet are pointing in while your upper legs are pushing
out. This position combined with the inner dynamic
tension you are generating with your upper legs will
give you a strong sense of being connected to the earth.

It will also form a sprung base from which to reinforce the power of your arms.

2 Extend one arm forward at a 45-degree angle so that your upper arm crosses your chest and your hand aims out of the centre of your chest toward the aggressor's nose. Keep the extended arm slightly bent at the elbow for resilience. Put your mental focus into the tip of your middle finger. Meanwhile, bring your other hand toward your extended arm's elbow. Keep the middle finger of this back-up hand pointing toward the bend of your extended arm's elbow. It should feel as though your arms are melded together as a strong shield.

3 Stand against a wall or in a corner so that you simulate being in a tight space. Ask your partner to begin directing punches toward your head and solar plexus region, slowly at first until you build up confidence. Deflect the punch and then immediately bring both hands back to centre to their original *neutral* position, so that you are prepared to deflect the next punch. The action is: deflect, recentre, deflect, recentre, and so on. DO NOT LOOK AT YOUR PARTNER'S ARMS. KEEP YOUR EYES ON YOUR PARTNER'S FACE AT ALL TIMES. ESPECIALLY WATCH THEIR EYES! After a while you will be able to sense the punch before your partner actually strikes at you.

At this time, and when you are fed up with deflecting, you may explore turning your extended protective open hand into a fist and striking them as your radar-like hands sense the right moment. This action of defence becoming counter-attack within a split second is also similar to fencing, where the fencer parries and then immediately ripostes. Sensing the opening in Wing Tsun is likened to a stop thrust or time thrust in the art of fencing. Here the fencer seems to read the mind of the opponent and counter-attacks just before the opponent has a chance to attack. With regular practice one can become proficient with the Wing Tsun idea of defence and counter-attack fairly quickly. This is one of its advantages. If the aggressor is too close, you could pretend to 'submit', putting a hand around the back of his neck. Once he has relaxed, you may then use the punch to its full, devastating effect, while pulling his head towards your fist for even greater impact.

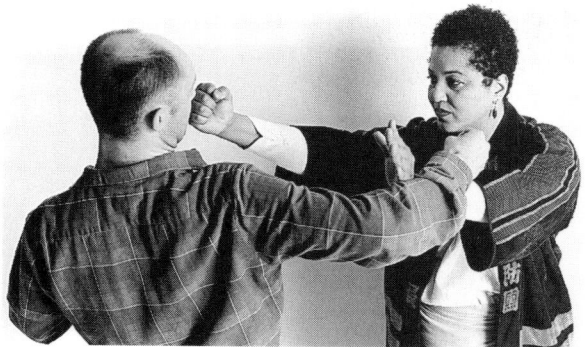

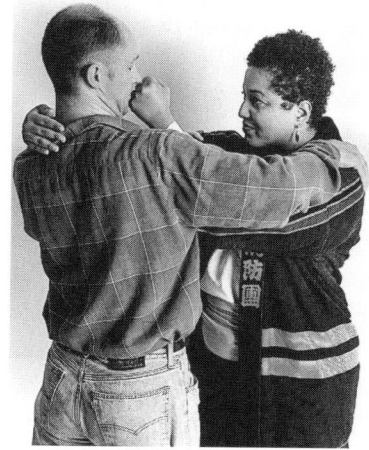

When you have become proficient and confident doing the 'on-guard' position from a static position, you may incorporate the technique into the confident advancing and retreating exercise which is at the beginning of this chapter. You may also practise using this technique for dealing with a coward who is trying to go around behind you by keeping your position relative to theirs by rotating your triangular stance so that you are always facing them.

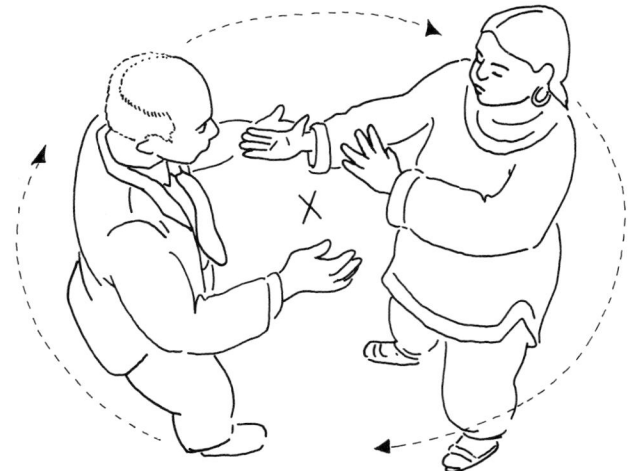

The defender (right) prevents the aggressive coward from getting behind her by following him and maintaining her protective on-guard strategy.

Well Suited for Women and Children

The Wing Tsun technique is particularly suitable for women and children. It can appear as though you are almost inviting the attacker in, rather like a cat hiding under a car to ambush a dog: when its opponent is caught in its trap, the cat attacks back. A woman can theatrically use her 'womanly wiles' to appear to be offering no resistance to the coward, and then, once she gains his confidence to the point that his guard is down, she can counter attack like a king cobra. So as you see, you can strategically use the element of surprise to draw your aggressor toward you to the point that they think they have you, and then extend your fist and arm as though through the centre of their face. Aim for the nose.

DEVELOPING INSTINCTIVE MOVEMENT: EVASION AND DIFFUSION TACTICS

The Elements: A Self-Contained Self-Preservation System

The use of the qualities of air, fire, water and earth is one of the most accessible approaches I use in my self-defence system. Building on the combination of self-esteem, body language and intuition, the elements represent a tangible spontaneous extraction of many years of martial arts training. They also express the philosophical and psychological base for this natural style of self-defence.

The elements offer access to many natural responses as a means of maintaining your power and its rightful space to express it. To prepare yourself on a mental/emotional level to gain the most from this system of self-defence, ask yourself the following questions:

Q: Is a wave trying to hit someone or something when it expresses the power of its nature?

A: No. It is just being true to the rhythm of its nature.

Q: Does the sun try to burn anything that interferes with its radiance?

A: No. It is simply radiating.

Q: Is the wind trying to knock someone over when it blows?

A: No. It is an ecological response to a change in air pressure.

Q: Is a mountain being stubborn when it won't move because someone is trying to push it?

A: No. It is just being.

Q: Is the earth angry when it moves?

A: You supply the answer.

These elements naturally surround us every day in the sunshine, the sea, the air and the earth that we inhabit, and they are in us. Along with metal and wood they constitute the categories for diagnosis and treatment in the Chinese medical system. The function of the heart and small intestines is *fire* and the ability to discriminate; *metal* and *air* relate to respiration and elimination – participation, inner strength, decisiveness and letting go; *earth* encompasses the functions of the stomach and spleen for grounding and building nourishment for the body/mind; *wood* goes with the liver and gall-bladder whose major functions include planning, and *water* describes the functions of the kidneys and bladder for flow and that soft power that is capable of cutting through mountains.

With this physically-based system one might venture the logic that we are essentially a microcosm of the elements. Our bodies are composed of them.

The Elements as Backbone to Our Emotions

The elements describe our emotions, as in the saying, 'He/she has a *fiery* personality. If we pay attention to this simple information we can use the elements to improve our instinctive power, in both our creative pursuits and in the context of self-defence. The elements can be used to bring you into contact with your emotions. If you are shy, you can access fire in yourself, or the strongest element which may very well be water. When you access the relevant element you can express yourself more spontaneously and to greater effect. Because of the simplicity of the elements, seemingly weaker people like women, children and the elderly have used them with a great deal of success.

I remember after the television series, *Stand Your Ground*, I was happy to receive three particular letters which referred to the use of the viewers' successful use of the elements: two were from parents who said that their daughters had watched the young teenage woman using the element fire on television, and used it themselves to get away from a cowardly aggressor. The other was from an elderly woman who had used the fire element to free herself from a burglar in her flat. Her only complaint was that, having chased him out of her flat, she wasn't able to catch him!

1 Remember how animals and small children make themselves heavy when they do not wish to be moved? Feel yourself rooted to the ground.

2 To effectively communicate the fire element you must put it out through your eyes as well, whilst moving your hands quickly towards the coward's eyes in a shoo-away manner.

3 To feel the water's protective force move both arms in a continuous 'figure of eight' pattern from your centre (navel), moving over and under the coward's wrists until you are free. Remember, you can also use your legs (especially your forward leg and foot) for kicking the aggressor's knee or stamping on their forward foot.

4 Make yourself light, elusive and forceful like the wind, whilst keeping connected to the ground through your feet and legs.

Become the Element

Though you may use your imaginary opponent in this exercise, it is important to receive feedback from a real person at some point.

1 In each of the elements make a mental list of its qualities such as hot, unpredictable, sparky and intense for fire, and light, invisible, omnipresent for air. Then spend *one minute* on your own *with each element* becoming its qualities. *Becoming the element* is the secret to the success of its use. If you merely pretend you keep yourself separate from its power. By becoming fire or earth you *are* its power.

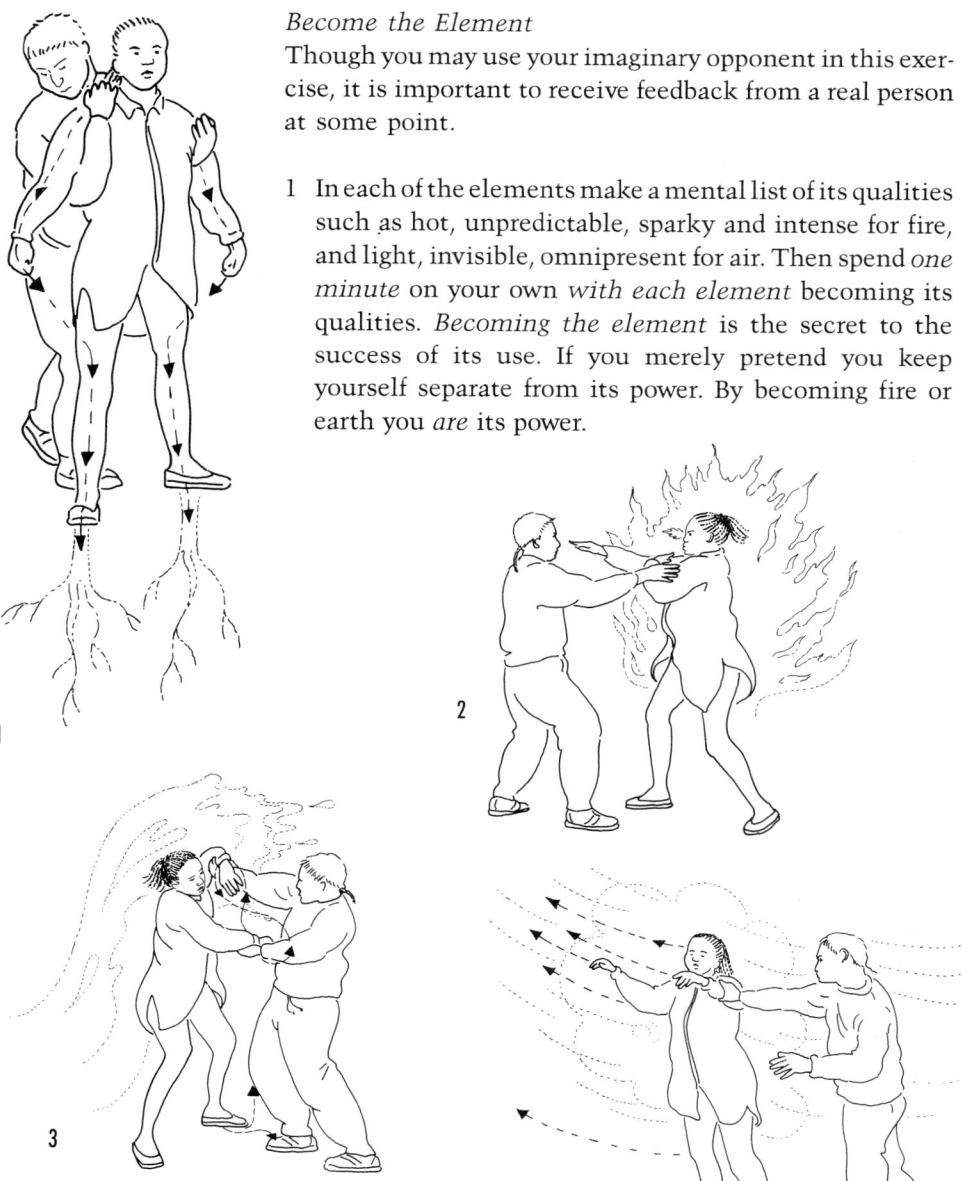

2 Keep the resilient arm feeling alive throughout the exercise and, in a way, add the element to this feeling as though you are draping a garment on it. You are now ready to go to the next step.

3 Be prepared to sense your partner's movement and to move toward them as though to take over their territory. Throughout this action aspect of the exercise keep your hands directed to the opponent's face. This will allow you to have more space so that you are less likely to slump into a victim's body language. It will also enable your body to express your intent more fully. Just like creating inner space for your emotions, ideas and values, **creating physical space makes room for a stronger, more balanced and accurate technique.**

Be aware of your footwork. Move in toward your opponent in a shuffle step. Slide along as though there is elastic between your feet. Remember: there are movements that involve crossing the legs in Kung Fu as a set-up movement for counter attack, but unless you are crossing your legs intentionally you might end up tripping yourself.

4 Having moved in each of the elements you may find that you feel more natural and powerful with one or two rather more than the others. This is natural. The element may characterize and reflect our strengths and weaknesses. Some of us feel strongest in our philosophical or *airy* element (not to be confused with airy-fairy spaciness), some are more powerful in the water element in our abilities to sense and mitigate the harsher aspects of life and personal interactions. Others of us may feel in our element in the direct intensity and spontaneity of fire. Still others of us radiate strength in our earthy abilities to organize practical details and so we may find more functionability in the stabilizing earth element.

You may find that you are comfortable in different elements for different areas of life. In any case, enjoy these awarenesses, then return to the context of self-protection and the most appropriate style for you when you think of protecting yourself. Focus on the ones that naturally work for you. Beyond this, if you'd like to expand your repertoire of elements in self-defence or any other areas, you may venture out at your leisure.

Many find fire to be a useful defence tactic because it allows you to feel the fiery nature of fear and anger, and at the same time, it allows you to constructively direct both of these emotions.

The Elements at the Transpersonal Level

The meaning of transpersonal in the context of self-defence is the ability to interact with something or someone in a neutral, dispassionate way. The only motive involved is to be a fair witness. The notion of focussing one's emotional and physical energy to hurt someone else is a limited expression. It may work sometimes, but the person who expresses themselves with the motive to maintain balance is the more powerful. When one acts out verbally, emotionally or physically as an attempt to remain true to one's own nature, outwardly-directed movements . such as punching, kicking or moving like fire are magnified versions of one's inner radiance.

When one is acting from this point of view, even in an attack situation rather than merely to attack or hurt back, one's power is limitless. This is why it is important to become the elements rather than to use them only to hurt.

I have learned over many years how powerful this concept is. I have had people use dirty tricks, to try to sabotage meaningful projects that I have set up. At first I was in shock that people would be that insecure that they would need to do such a silly thing. Then when I realized that it was one of the limited ways of the human condition, I've learned that the best retaliation is simply to get out of the way and let the consequences of their actions be taken care of by the mirror of karma ('what we sow, we reap'). And how quickly it works when I get out of the way. This approach has greatly reinforced my self-esteem. There have been many times that people's attitudes were saying to me, 'No, you won't ever get a college education', or, 'You can't do that. You're not the right colour, gender, class, or age, and besides, it's already been done before.' At first this bothered me. Now, when I am in touch with the fire, water, earth and air of myself, I see these demeaning attitudes are but reflections of how limited or unknowledgeable these people are, and I move on to those who are much more astute. This is acting at the transpersonal level, i.e. not taking other people's problems personally.

Basic Confidence When Dealing With More Than One Coward

It is enough to consider being attacked by one coward. The potential threat of more than one attacker can feel completely overwhelming. The chances of escaping can seem very slim indeed. There is hope though. You must begin by demystifying the reasons why cowards attack in numbers. All of the self-defence strategies begin with a mental strength which is based on self-worth.

Most attacking cowards have power where they feel they can remain anonymous. This is why so many of them have to hide behind masks and why they find the need to attack in dark alleys, or when they think no one else is in the house. It is a known fact that rapists try to shut up their targets by covering their mouths or by hiding behind a lethal weapon. Perpetrators of incest threaten with: 'Don't you tell anyone.' Somewhere they know they are ill and that their action is cowardly so they use threats to keep from being discovered.

When there is the need for others to support the cowards in their ill-founded behaviour, they are really saying that the person they think they can attack is much more than they can handle alone, so they need more of their kind to complete the action. The more members needed in gangs, the more power they are unwittingly giving away to the person they hope to attack. It is important in considering how to deal with more than one attacking coward to realize this and then mentally to seize the power they are giving you. When rehearsing an attack situation with more than one opponent take the following steps:

1 Even though there are more of them than you, you can treat them as one unit who you are capable of organizing. Mobs tend to be composed of one leader, the leader's side-kick, and the rest are followers who are either attempting to build up their tough image, or they are so weak on their own that they simply follow. Take an overview of the oncoming mob and look for the so-called leader. Then look for exit points before they get near you. Rehearse the possibility of being surrounded by them. To exit use the side of your body as a knife edge. Again, be aware of your footwork, as crossing your feet will hamper your ability to exit efficiently.

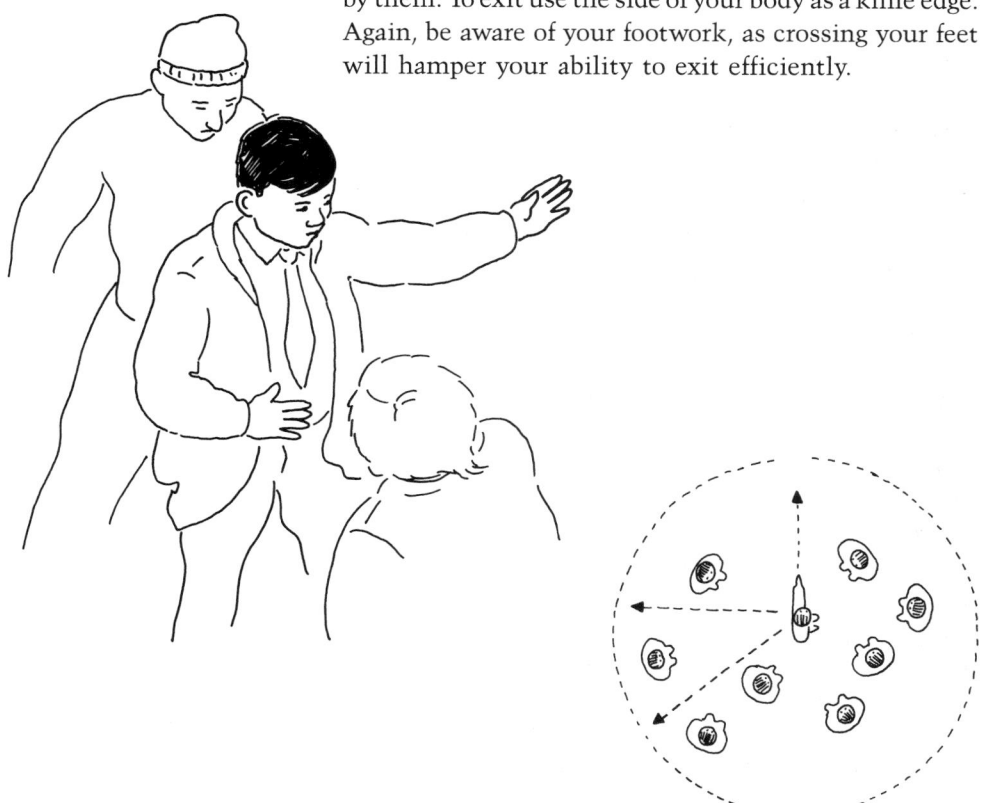

The illustrations demonstrate a way to practise finding your exit points in the event of being suddenly surrounded by a cowardly gang. The diffusion of aggression is made expedient by exiting near the leader. It is important in this exercise to try to keep still even though you may be naturally afraid. The stillness will enable you to perceive and move in a more confident way.

In dealing with any self-defence rehearsal, it is crucial in the training to consider:

1 How did you get into the situation?
2 What were the circumstances that led to you being in this situation?

These questions may sound like they are designed to blame the victim, but they are not. When we are privileged to be able to rehearse self-protective tactics in a safe place, each of these questions improves awareness. These questions describe in practice the maxim, 'an ounce of prevention is worth a pound of cure'. Given this awareness through the questions surrounding the circumstances of an attack, you may find that you can prevent many of the 'what ifs' you have been worried about.

Key Points for Evasion
1 Look for the weaknesses in grips.

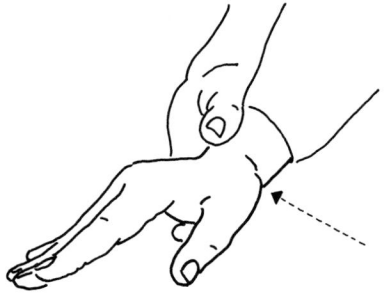

2 Look for the gaps in the person.

3 Look for the gaps in
a crowd or mob situation.

4 Look for exits in
buildings (windows, doors).

5 Look for things in your immediate
environment you can use to your advantage.

The Spiralling Pillar of Fire

One of the considerations that may come up in your rehearsal is what to do if you don't exit and more than one of these cowards grab you. This is a good point. There are a number of options available to you. You can stand there and let them grab you. You can offer your 'resilient arms' to them so that you are in a much stronger position for your next move – sort of attracting the flies to the honey (there are only so many of their hands that can fit onto your arms). Once you have them where you want them you can reorganize them by becoming the centre. They will be disadvantaged by your power rather than you being the victim of theirs. This type of response requires you to establish a comfortable feeling with aggressive people being close to you. You can duck under them. You can act as though you are mad. You can scream for help.

If they strike or kick at you, you can use the Wing Tsun defence principle in a revolving manner.

All of these are certainly options, though I recommend a tactic that is strategic and effective. Part of being confident is feeling radiant in your fullness. Out of this fullness you may express the fiery, airy, watery and earthy elements of your radiance.

People are more afraid of nature, such as the power of the sea or of wild animals, than of other human beings because many arrogantly believe we are superior to nature. Nature is a great teacher of the element of surprise. Unless we have full knowledge of the way a volcano erupts, or where a hurricane will hit within a town, or how high a tidal wave will rise we simply cannot control these events. Even though a scientist may have enough facts to determine probability, the 'new' science of chaos is shaking up a lot of traditional theories. Nature is full of these surprises. Some of us freak out at seeing something much smaller than us, like spiders, because we can't predict what they will do next. The use of nature as an extension of our radiance is a powerful strategy in self-defence.

We will explore becoming various animals in the next chapter on safety. For now, the pillar of rapidly-spiralling fire is a potent tool in dealing with more than one attacker. A certain amount of structuring is required to ensure the success of this technique.

Keep your shoulders relaxed and elbows out from your body. As you do this firmly press your strength into the points of your elbows so that they are full of your mental strength. Now keeping your elbows out and up just below shoulder level twist as far as you can one way and then the other.

Escaping From More Than One Coward: the Confident Approach
You will need a minimum of two willing helpers for this exercise.

1 Ask your partners to stand on either side of you. Now have them grab your arms with the intent to take you away somewhere.

2 Using the principle of judo, walk with them to minimize the feeling of pressure you will be receiving from them. In fact, you might explore walking just slightly faster than them, though not so fast that they catch on to the fact that you are taking over the lead. With them on either side of you, feel how they have lost some of their own integrity. They may even be the puppets of someone else. And though they may seem imposing they are weak because they are not acting with integrity. Remember, they think you are more powerful than either of them; that's why they need to back each other up.

3 There is a point where they will begin to converge toward their immediate destination. It may be a getaway car, a door or another thug. You will know this moment through your strongest sense, as described in Chapter 2. At this moment, firmly grasp your wrist and activate your spiralling pillar of fire by twisting. Twist like the agitating motion of the insides of a washing machine. Notice your extended elbows conveniently move to their vulnerable areas. The protection of their vulnerable areas, combined with your 'supernatural' and unpredictable motion will weaken their hold on you.

4 Explore throwing them into each other. Ironically, the more the merrier in this situation. This is because there are many of them and only so much of you that they can grab at any one time. Your confident centrifugal motion will separate the weak from the strong. You are strong in your radiance of your rightful space.

Exiting a Gang of Cowards Who Encircle You

One of the elements of surprise that can be used by organized cowards is plotting to encircle you. Once again, this is a real signal that they are very weak on their own, so they find it necessary to intimidate by encircling.

This is often the case in large cities where lost and desperate teenagers and even children find ways to mug for money or to intimidate 'for kicks' as a means of seeking the internal balance they are lacking. The first step in dealing with this type of situation is to be aware that it happens. A man recently told me how he remembered watching the local gangs of ten-to-thirteen year olds in New York as they circled the people who had just arrived from Long Island. Many of the Long Islanders were visiting because they had tickets for concerts and the opera. The gangs knew this, and before the unsuspecting visitor knew what hit them, their pockets would be empty and the gangs would have a hefty income for weeks to come as a result of scalping the expensive tickets. The man who told me about this said that even though he used to watch this nefarious enterprise from the window of his high-rise apartment, he was not immune to being a potential victim himself. However, because he was aware that this style of organized mugging took place he had the advantage over one who was completely innocent to the street ways of the locals.

One day he was walking in the neighbourhood when he found that he was being slowly surrounded. At the moment that he felt the circle forming he distracted the gang by asking, 'Got any small change?' His question was met with, 'No, get out of here, kid!'

I thought this was a brilliant response, and, in a way, one could say he was using the Wing Tsun principle in a street-wise and vocal way. What he effectively did was intercept the cowards' potential attack by holding up a mirror to the gang and giving them a reflection of their own actions. He spoke their language, and most cowards do not like to have done to them what they do to others. This is part of the cowardly equation:

Cowardly success = ability to remain anonymous;
Cowardly exposure = loss of power to succeed.

OVERVIEW

In order to be effective at anything we do, we need to be confident and calm. Out of confidence comes our ability to be spontaneous and resourceful in dealing with all challenging situations.

CHECKLIST

☑ **Centre Line** Be aware of the centre line of your body as you walk, sit, stand, when lying down, in exercise and in speaking. Your centre line will focus your mental and physical energies and will minimize fragmentation of your concentration.

☑ **Stamina** Practise chain punching with a target in mind (as described in this chapter). In addition to improving your concentration, this exercise will build stamina. Stamina reinforces your confidence as it produces an emotional feeling of being able 'to go the distance'.

☑ **The Elements** Make use of the elements as an immediate way of organizing your mental, physical and emotional energies for both purposes of dealing with threatening situations as well as for expressing yourself fully as you canny out the activities of your day.

☑ **Dealing With More Than One Attacking Coward** Do not fragment your power. Treat the group as one irritating force. If you are surrounded by a group, find the exit routes. If you cannot get through the exit routes, look for people and things in your immediate environment that you can use to your advantage. Use the 'Spiralling Pillar of Fire' motion, twisting and turning like the agitator in a washing machine to disperse the organization of the mob, and then make use of the elements and the Wing-Tsun defensive/offensive strategy.

AFFIRMATION

I handle every situation with ease. I am resourceful.

4 | **The Fourth Dimension**

THE REALM OF SAFETY

In this chapter we will work with the most obvious need for self-defence: safety. Building on the lessons presented in the previous three chapters these guidelines are a plan of action for responding to the possibility of violence in day-to-day situations.

Being confident means being aware of the value of your life. After all we each have a unique purpose and destiny. It is, however, sometimes much easier to think of the safety of others first. This is especially true of women. We have been conditioned to be the ones who take care. Before we consider the way we feel about a situation, much more 'ladylike' phrases roll easily off our tongues such as:

'Do you have enough?'

'What do you think?'

'Where should we go?'

'Oh I know he's a pain, but I don't want to hurt his feelings.'

All very nice, but potentially deadly when we choose to ignore our ability to discriminate between the right and the wrong time to extend courtesy to others. Although there is an admirable degree of politeness in these considerations, and they certainly enhance our social skills, these considerations can cost us our lives in a life-or-death situation. When 'being nice' *all the time* becomes a knee-jerk habit, it will slow us down if we are called to protect our well-being and that of those we love.

On the other hand, the same maternal instincts that lead women to ask the above questions can be externalized and can turn one into a vicious lioness when loved ones are threatened. But how many of us would do it for ourselves?

Our levels of self-esteem, inner strength, and being confident determines the answer to this question. At the root of self-esteem, inner strength, etc. is one's ability to defend oneself. Each of us has our individual styles for different dangerous situations: running away; fighting back; picking our noses; verbally fighting back; evasion, are among the many.

In this chapter we will explore the use of our body/mind weapons. The information presented in the 14 steps will prescribe a distilled repertoire to reinforce your natural self-defence ability and minimize vulnerability to aggressive cowards.

DRUG AND ALCOHOL ABUSE – A ROOT OF MUCH EVIL

Myth: People who attack are sex-crazed or genetically predisposed to aggression.

Fact: Eighty per cent of domestic and public violence world-wide is caused by drug and/or alcohol abuse. In Chapter 1 we looked at the internal affairs that motivate an attacker. While the need to control and dominate may be passed on from our parents, another social cloud certainly encourages this lack of self-esteem. When this internal balance is not recognized and dealt with in constructive ways, the gap is wide open for other distracting and destructive means of anaesthetizing the pain.

Drugs and habitual alcohol use are 'pain killers' that are socially reinforced. They are even referred to as social lubricants in some circles. Some drugs may be prescribed to create a chemical balance where there is no other means of fulfilling the deficiency, but the evils of, for example, cocaine, speed, LSD, crack and excessive alcohol are extensive. Look at the news every night. Vehicular collisions; child abuse and other forms of domestic violence such as battered and raped wives; murders; rape in general; the raping and pillaging that occur during wars; environmental disasters such as the massive oil spillages which kill and destroy the homes of thousands upon thousands of innocent creatures – they are so often committed by people who are victims of drug/alcohol abuse, either personally or through parents. A good friend of mine who lives in San Francisco says that the sound of multiple gun shots from the crack dealers across the road from her are part of the street sounds every evening. This sort of thing was once an isolated, terrifying event. Now it is 'normal'. And the bad news is that it is on the increase.

Seeds of Our Future

It was recently reported that drug and alcohol use among 10–13 year olds has risen by 80 per cent over the last five years. It is once again becoming the 'in thing' among young teenagers and students. They cruise pharmacies to buy or steal any kind of drug from aspirin to cold tablets and cough medicine to get their hourly buzz, their escape from the real problems. In the last year there has been a 20 per cent increase in the use of hallucinogens and inhalants. One out of three drink alcohol on a daily basis. One out of four smoke cigarettes. These statistics reflect only one segment of society – 10–13 year olds. They are our future.

What Signals to Look for in Drug and Alcohol Abusers

As the statistics show, most violence occurs as a result of drugs and alcohol. Given this fact, if you want to enter into self-defence with a comprehensive awareness I recommend that you take a look at the following symptoms in anyone who tries to interfere with your well-being. This information will strengthen your understanding in the event of a violent confrontation, and in so doing, will give you more of an edge in your choice of response because you will effectively be demystifying the attacker. If you find any of these signals to be familiar in the behaviour of loved ones, those you work with, or even in yourself, it will lead to a better understanding of why they or you behave in a particular way. You might be able to encourage them to get help in the right way and with the best and safest timing.

If you find these signals to be chronically present in you or a friend or colleague and you are surprised because neither you nor they take drugs or drink excessively, they may signal that somewhere you or they are harbouring debilitating fear or are in pain to such a dangerous degree that these symptoms are being exhibited in order to escape the real source of your discomfort. Perhaps you are in a relationship that is hurtful to you or in work that is not fulfilling. Awareness is the first step to healing yourself and seeking the help you may need to change these aspects of your life into something more fulfilling. This knowledge alone is empowering.

Some of the signals are: dilated pupils; glazed, reddened and unfocussed eyes; disorientation; blisters around the nose; lack of muscular coordination; a chemical odour; strange stains on clothing; slurred speech; uncontrollable giggling; stomach and muscle cramps; excessive coughing and sniffing; sleeping problems; reduced appetite; decreased or increased sexual drive; erratic communication; mood swings; emotional extremes.

Government and Community Intervention

I do not doubt that much of this problem could be eradicated if the government would take a closer look at the source of the problem and implement this awareness in the educational system. To get through the 'natural rebellion' excuse, this educational reform would have to go beyond the blanket warnings of do's and don'ts. A three-part programme would be a more viable warning.

1 An assertive exposé of the rampancy and ramifications of the abuse of alcohol and drugs would start the educational process.
2 A deeper understanding and a clearer explanation of the reasons that underlay all forms of abuse.
3 This education would have to offer alternative, healthy ways to have fun while building self-esteem; and it would have to take into account the value of the

uniqueness of the individual, to insist upon structuring ways to access individual aptitude, rather than simply shuttling everyone off into the sports arena in order to *build character*. This would require teachers who have put the spotlight on their own self-esteem to find the best mode of communicating these values. I got bored and disenchanted too as a teenager when, in the face of a teacher shortage we were subjected to learning a very distorted and comical version of world history by a football coach. He was stretched beyond his abilities in what was clearly not his field – all of the children were aware that he didn't know what he was talking about, but we had to put up with him. Unfortunately this is often the case where a child's awareness is stifled in favour of the adult who is lacking skills or internal resources.

The only way that change will happen is when students and parents alike demand that education about the whole notion of abuse comes out of the closet and becomes an integral part of the education process in general.

There is hope for change in the face of this looming drug machine. I'd like to share a song which was written by a twelve-year old named Summer Diane Jones. Sung in the modern *hip-hop* rhythm, the song describes a young girl who fell victim to the drug scene. It is both a plea for help and a riveting exposé of the consciousness that is dawning on the youth of today. The will to change is there. What is needed is our concentrated help on a family, community and national scale:

Can You See What I'm Talking 'Bout?
SUMMER DIANE JONES, AGE 12

I'm going to tell you something today, we're all going to make it in a special way.
See we're going to get help but ya gotta help too, or else you're gonna be something, and that's – through.

We can't make it in this world on our own, we can't be like
E.T. and always phone home.

So we gotta be all that we can be and do all we can do. That's
what God sent us on this earth to do.

And now you're going to find out what I'm talking 'bout,
it's time for you to jump up and scream and shout.

You've gotta shout freedom, to speak, to learn, to even be
a scum.

The freedom to speak, the freedom to learn, that is the
freedom that we shouldn't have to earn.

In the summertime we had a vacation, now it's time for
us to come back for our education.

Can you see what I'm talking 'bout, you've got to get it
straight?

Can you see what I'm talking 'bout before it is too late?

You've got to get it through your head the feeling ain't that
great.

Can you see what I'm talking bout?

Can you see before it is too late?

There was a girl and her name was Veronica. When she was
little she wanted to play the Harmonica.

But then she got a little older and wanted to play with
something a little bolder, come to find out no one ever
told her

About drugs, how they can make you feel like you're the
only bug, the only slug, the only rug.

When she found out it was a little too late, cause when she
did she was past the gate.

Veronica, she had a baby, and when it came out it was
active as gravy.

Her baby was dead, and she let it go to her head. Then she
said, 'I'm glad that my baby's dead . . . I couldn't handle
it anyways.

That baby would always be in my darn way. I don't have
time for an extra behind, I hardly have enough for myself
to survive.

I aint a cat and I aint Bart Simpson . . . I really wish that
I could get a glimpse

In my future, to see what other torture is to come of me -
tell me oh what shall I be?'

I really don't know. You could be outside hustling in the
snow saying,

'I sell drugs, need some?' But take it from me, you don't
want none.

It will make your life hell, your head will be ringing like
a bell, and soon as you know you'll be in jail.

So save your life and be smart, don't even get yourself into
a mess like this from the start.

And by the way, Veronica was thirteen, now wasn't that a
situation for her to see.

Oh Veronica, now she's dead. This whole situation straight
blew up her head.

So you see, don't ever let this happen to you or me. Stay
in school. Don't be a fool. Listen to Bobby Brown and
don't be cruel.

(Chorus)

Your life will flash right before your eyes, and we'll be
looking down with tears in our eyes,

Saying, 'It wasn't your fault, you shouldn't have died. It was
the parents fault, they should have told you ahead of
time.'

Now this is how the story ends. Don't let your life be like
a money bin.

You always give and you never stop, then one day you're
going to take and going to drop.

So keep it in mind, and keep yourself ahead of time, cause
we don't want to see none of you all die.

Peace.

Self-Esteem Revisited

The motivation for most cowardly attacks is the perpetrators' unconscious need to gain control of some area of vulnerability inside themselves. This is because they know they are out of control through their fear of being vulnerable. As they are lacking in the courage or know-how to tackle the real problem within themselves, they look for people to attack instead. They are so damaged and so out of balance that, because their self-esteem wallet is empty, they try to restore this level of personal power by getting it from outside themselves.

As it was mentioned above, drug and alcohol abuse are the source many of these aggressive attempts to restore inner balance. In this light it seems that attacking others who either show signs of vulnerability or those who are confident in their lives is the next step in the unbalanced person's ill-fated search for personal security.

Step one in counteracting these sick people is to cultivate this awareness of why they attack. This awareness will minimize the initial debilitating shock that can be such a vivid part of the 'victim'. That is, it can take it out of the personal realm, out of *blaming the victim* with the hurtful and horrifying feeling of, 'Why are they doing this to me? What did I do to *cause* them to treat me this way', and change it back into the real problem: 'Why are they doing this to themselves? I refuse to let them do this to me'. (This must be an internal feeling first and foremost. It can, of course, be expressed verbally if, after evaluating the situation, you feel safe to do so.)

No matter how imposing or powerful they may seem, all people who attack, tall and muscular or short and stout, bare-faced or masked, male or female, are suffering a deficiency in their self-esteem. This is true of those who molest, rape, steal, vandalize, batter and murder.

More and More Are Being Caught

I am happy to see that more and more of these cowards who feel the need to attack are being caught and exposed for what they are. For some reason it seems much more profitable for the media to report the horrible situations rather than the successful defusion of violent and potentially violent situations.

The truth is that there are more successful escapes than there are actual attacks. Here is an example of one such success which exposes the seemingly powerful, menacing rapist as the coward that he really is. The story takes place in a small town in the US where a man raped women much smaller than himself. These were all women who lived on their own. The coward lurked around neighbourhoods and studied homes that had been recently vacated and watched to see if a single woman moved in. These are the people he targeted. He especially targeted women who had recently moved into single-story houses with single-paned windows. Even though many of them were cautious to keep their windows closed when they left for work, he managed to sneak around during the day to cut the glass near the lock so that he could gain access at a time in the night when they were sleeping and, seemingly, most vulnerable.

After several rapes a police officer began to detect the coward's mode of operation. So he predicted the next likely woman who would be targeted, one who had just moved into a one-story house with single-paned windows. The heroine in this story is a woman police officer who courageously chose to pretend to be the woman the coward was stalking. It was fortunate that she bore a striking resemblance to the new woman in the neighbourhood.

It took several nights for the coward to attack the heroine, who was waiting for him in bed, but when he did there were two male officers in the closet, and several on watch outside who radioed to the officers inside to warn them. The coward, who masqueraded as a macho stud wet his pants and sobbed like a baby, while he pleaded: 'Please, please, don't hurt me.' The male officers were disgusted. One of them sarcastically yelled in his face: 'What a big,

big man you are. You're disgusting, and you're gonna pay for it!'

The apprehension of such cowards is on the increase. Much of this is to do with the male officers who are taking violence toward women more seriously. The result is a tougher position on abolishing this cowardly act. It is also to do with the higher profile of women in the police force, and their courageous willingness to set themselves up in the likely path of the aggressive cowards.

Every attacker is vulnerable somewhere. The next exercise will help you detect these weaknesses so that you may either defuse their aggression before it becomes dangerous to you or, if the situation escalates to a dangerous stage, you may plot the moment which feels safe to respond appropriately (reminder: appropriate = what feels right for you at that particular time).

Detecting the Weakness: Who are the Potential Cowards?
You will need 3–5 friends or willing helpers, and a few hours to enjoy the value of the exercise. Everyone in the group can benefit from the exercise as it:

improves sensitivity to both the intent and the weakness in the cowardly attacker(s).
improves your sense of timing for escaping or diffusing a violent situation.
educates you in recognizing your own stereotypes of those who are likely attackers. These stereotypes can leave you off-guard.

1 Have a brainstorming session and form two written lists. Label the left-hand column *possible cowardly attackers,* and the right-hand column *possible places.* Try to compile a written list of as many faces a cowardly attacker can possibly take.
2 All but one of you will get into the role of attackers you have chosen from the first column. (If possible make

this as theatrical as you can. Use make-up and have everyone dress up in their respective roles.)

When everyone is in character, have them choose two out of the group who will be the cowards. One will simply think malicious intentions toward you. The other will be contemplating attacking you. Those who remain can either be neutral or well-wishers.

3   Have everyone form a large circle. They are to keep their roles secret so that you may walk around and discriminate the attackers from the neutral ones or allies.

4   After you have announced your revelations, discuss why you picked up what you did from each person. You might have noticed that the ones with ill intent were breathing in a shallow way, or seemed cold or uneasy, while those with good will were warmer, more radiant and, generally, exuded a good atmosphere. Maybe the potentially aggressive ones seemed out of balance in their bodies with sunken chest (an indication of low self-esteem) or hyper-extended chest, clinched fists, or jutting jaws (all defensive postures). These are indications of their vulnerable areas. Someone who is cold is locked up inside and, given the fire of your inner strength, they can be toppled. Those with sunken chests can be pushed over. Those with hyper-extended chests and jaws can be pulled or lured off-balance.

Don't worry if you weren't accurate the first time around. The purpose of this exercise is to give everyone a chance to practise and become better at it. This is your privilege.

5   Now let everyone in the group have a chance to play detective.

6   Make plans to meet regularly until all of you become confident with your ability to detect the potential cowardly attackers. The real feedback to your confidence will come when you use your skill in the 'field', outside the safety of your homes.

7 Once you become proficient in your sensitivity, do the
same practice with blindfolds. Also, extend your lists of
likely attackers and places to more and more obscure
and subtle possibilities. This exercise will sharpen you
intuition. Practise it regularly until you feel confident
with its purpose.

Your Flight Distance

The next tactical skill in the self-defence safety realm is
something I borrowed from nature. It relates to human
attempts to tame wolves in the wild. (The unquestioned,
deeply-seated insecurity in many men has heretofore given
them the permission to attempt to 'conquer nature'. Such
an arrogant assumption when even the flight of such a
small creature as a butterfly can wreak havoc with highly
scientific weather predicting machinery, not to mention
the fact that droughts, floods, earthquakes and pestilence
are capable of conquering humans in moments.)

Wolves who have been in the wild from birth are
virtually untameable. They maintain a 'flight distance'
when they are approached by humans. This flight distance
is particularly apparent in the female of the species and
ranges from 10 to 20 feet. The conscious distance works
as a double-edged detecting device; it allows them to
interact with humans if they are interested, it also serves
as a head-start if the wolf becomes threatened by the
human. They seem to have a built-in sense of the
importance of utilizing space in their forward plan of
escape. And given that most attackers are out to conquer,
humiliate and dominate, this approach to safety seems a
good place to start.

Flight distance gives the one who is being pursued the
benefit of handicap. Anyone who drives will recognise this
flight distance as part of a driver's education, where we are
encouraged to maintain a distance of at least one car's
length for every ten miles of speed. This space provides
more time to respond and maximizes the probability of
escape from collision if something were to suddenly

interfere with the flow of traffic. The analogy to driving may not be so irrelevant. After all, driving has to do with reaching a destination, and when we are in the stream of our purpose, whether it be immediate or long-term, each of us is moving within the whole container of our body/mind/presence to maintain our well-being whilst we reach our goals. On a more immediate level we practise flight distance when we plan ahead in any area.

Get Your Flight Distance

1 Establish your awareness of the distance at which you would feel safe if attacked in various situations, such as at a bus stop, in a bus, in your car, in the office, etc. Would it be two feet, five, twenty? Perhaps it would change with the setting. You may develop use of this flight distance simply by thinking and feeling in your daily settings. For instance, if you are at a phone booth, practise looking around you every 10 seconds. Use your peripheral vision. Not only will this improve your general awareness, it will also communicate to some coward who is fantasizing you as a target for their weakness that you are not an empty vacuum for their use.

2 Look for potential escape routes or people and things you could summon to your aid. Take a few moments to establish this wherever you are. How much of a radius do you have? Solely focusing straight ahead will limit your options for escape or opportunity. A circle with you in the centre is better. A sphere wherein you have the benefit of up and down response as well as front, back and to the sides opens many more possibilities. This will increase your chances of successful evasion, which is considered in the martial arts world to be the best self-defence. Your flight distance will also heighten your sensitivity to useful opportunities in your immediate environment.

3 Once you have established your flight distance, be aware that you are the organizing centre of that sphere, a calm

centre in the universe. Rather than being at the mercy of everything around your sphere, radiate your presence in all directions of the sphere. This is a high level Tai Chi concept which, when interpreted this way, can be immediately recognized as a spontaneous practical skill.

4 Once you feel comfortable in your flight-distance sphere, you can begin filling it with some of the techniques from all of the realms of this book, and you can certainly bring to it your own natural responses.

Not Without Accuracy

In the event that you are called to use physical technique to protect yourself, *the importance of accuracy cannot be stressed enough*. Technique without accuracy is nothing short of a pilot flying a plane without flying instructions, or a surgeon operating without knowledge of anatomy and physiology.

When I work with children and the wise ones over 60, accuracy is at the top of the list in practical self-defence skills, after self-worth and the righteous intent to protect what is most valuable to you. You may not feel particularly confident in a certain moment of crisis. You can get away with not being confident if you are accurate. Accuracy cuts through ambiguity and time/energy wasted in struggle.

Where to Strike

If you find that, in an attack situation, you have exhausted your evasion tactics and the coward still persists, you may have to counter attack as that may be the only language that the aggressive coward can understand. The best places to direct your intent are the following:

1 Up and under the NOSE

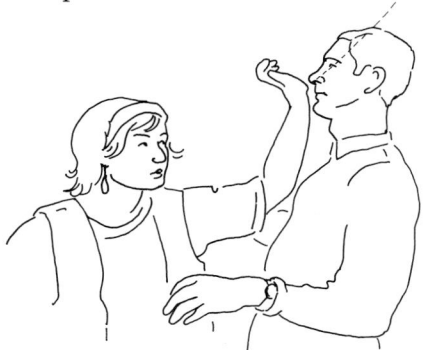

2 Up and under the CHIN

3 Into the EYES

4 Surrounding the THROAT; WINDPIPE and CAROTID ARTERIES

Grip with such a force that your thumb and other fingers meet around and behind the cowardly attacker's windpipe (trachea).

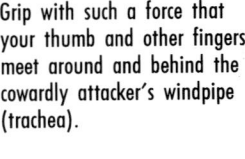

5 Under and up into the GROIN

6 Straight into the SHINS; if attacked from behind, use your heel to strike and scrape the shin

7 Down at a 45° degree angle and into the INSTEPS

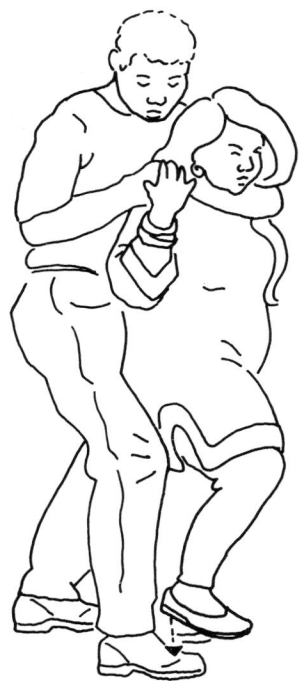

8 The LONG BONES and TOES

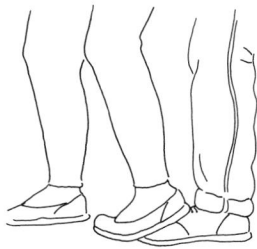

Memorize these areas and also be aware of them for your own protection against anyone who might attempt to attack you using any of these places on your body (see Wing Tsun idea, chapter 3).

YOUR STRATEGIC NATURAL WEAPONS

WARNING: **These techniques are very effective for the sole purposes of directing a cowardly attacker's attention away from you and back onto themselves. Any use of these weapons other than for self-protection could lead to serious repercussions and, therefore, unrelenting regret on your part.**

Obviously, there are many ways to use your body to protect yourself. We have all seen them at the movies. We will focus on the most effective ones listed below:

The Punch

Having mentioned the movies, most of us are familiar with the twisting punch associated with karate as a way of developing power. This is certainly a valuable skill to have, but in the event of a sudden attack it is better to use physical weapons that have natural power built into them. In punching, this natural power comes from the line in which you swing your arms as you walk. The arm swings to your sides with the palm facing inward.

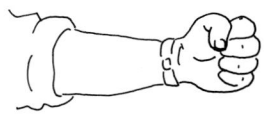

If you are striking with strong intent to the vital,

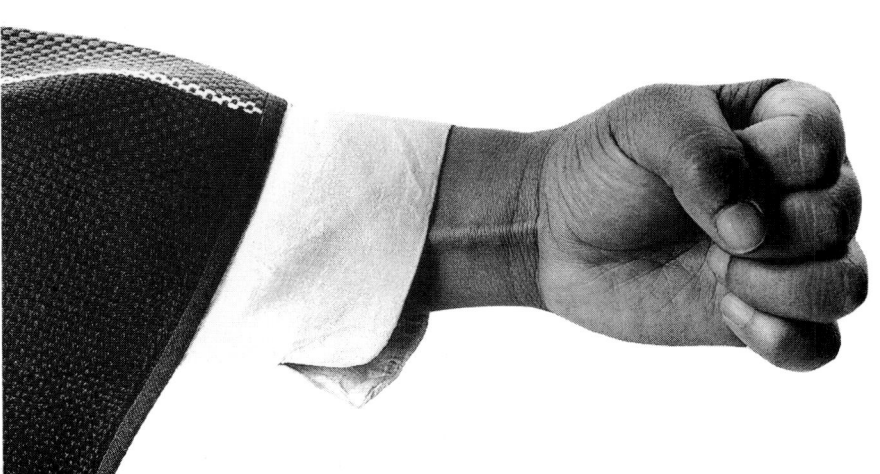

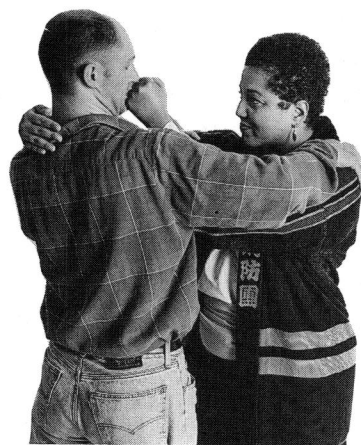

sensitive areas of a cowardly attacker you do not need twisting power. Though striking the pose may serve to impress the coward with your knowledge, it may also work against you by removing your element of surprise as you broadcast your intent to the attacker.

Squeeze and Sneeze Strategy for Punching
Shape your punching weapon by drawing your curled fingers to the centre of your palm. Wrap your thumb around the second section of your curled middle finger. Keep your wrist straight. Do not squeeze too tightly as you form your fist as this will tighten the viaducts of your power, i.e. your arms, shoulders and chest. These areas should be kept loose until the point of contact with your target. At the point of contact squeeze your fist and allow the power to exit your body like an explosive sneeze.

When punching, do not pull your elbow back to gather power. This will take too much time and it splits your power between front and back. Keep a positive, firm focus forward when directing it toward your target. This *principle of keeping your strike ahead of you* or *closer to the target* should apply to all the uses of your body/mind weapons. *The best target for the punch is up and under the nose.* Striking to the chest and abdomen may work on some but the nose area is vulnerable on everyone. The best approach is the Wing-Tsun approach described in chapter 3.

The Rocketing Heel of the Hand

This, and the following exercise can also be found in *Stand Your Ground*. I have included them here because they are so very essential to know and remember that I feel it is worthwhile to repeat them.

1 Using the principles of the squeeze and sneeze punch, keep your body relaxed, yet full of your intent until the point of release. Gather strength and power from the earth and your feet and legs to use the heel of your hand to strike up under the nose.
2 A slightly less serious retaliatory target for the rocketing heel of the hand is under the chin. Apply the same principles as above.

The Back of the Head to Attacker's Face

This weapon is useful when a cowardly aggressor attacks you from behind. (They are so weak inside that they can't even confront you face to face). Simply focus on the roundest part of the back of your head, especially the upper part of your head. Then mentally see it, and energetically feel it as a large sledge hammer (6 inches in diameter). Focus your anger, tighten your shoulders for support, feel the connection and strength of your feet and legs with the ground, and then decisively swing your head backwards through the face of the coward.

The Butterfly Choke

A weapon that will serve you when both the coward's hands are occupied with you is the butterfly choke. Remember anything they think they can do to you, you can do better in the use of this weapon. People with small and delicate hands will find this to be a particularly valuable alternative to counter choking a coward in the usual way.

1 Recognize the target areas, the trachea *windpipe* and the carotid arteries that supply blood and oxygen to the brain (necessary for living).

2 Wrap your hands like pliers around the aggressor's neck and sink your thumbs as deeply as you can above the Adam's apple, then squeeze your thumbs together as firmly as possible so that you feel them meet together around the coward's windpipe. You may give yourself even more strength by mentally thinking of your thumbs as though they are a smaller and more focused set of pliers.

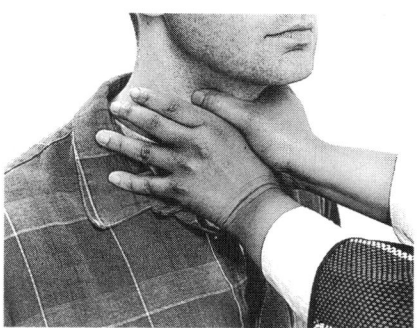

The Naked Arm Choke

This is a powerful suppressive technique from judo which is especially well suited for women, children and smaller-boned people in general.

1 To achieve successful use of this mental/physical weapon, use the sharp inner edge of your forearm near your wrist against the middle of the aggressor's throat. Slide your hands in a relaxed but quick manner around their neck.

2 Clasp your hands together so they make a secure square knot.

3 Press your chest into the aggressor's neck and drop your head along the side of their head.

4 Very firmly draw the sharp edge of your forearm in toward you so that you move halfway into the cross section of the neck. The aggressor will already begin to feel the pressure on their neck.

5 Keeping your head down and the pressure perpendicularly into their neck, scoop your choking arm up towards their head.

Your Machine Gun Elbow
Even though the aggressor may be pinning your arms to your sides, you can turn your head to aim for the solar plexus or groin and strike repeatedly as though your elbow were the multiple bullets of a machine gun. Try to avoid bringing your arm forward before you strike backwards. Again, the aggressor may sense what you are about to do, and this will leak the advantage of the element of surprise. Let your momentum develop within you with your righteous anger and then positively swing in the nearest line or curve to the attacker's vital area.

Aim under the kneecap, use the ground to give you strength, and keep one knee drawn in preparation to kick the other knee.

About Kicking

It is very exciting to both watch and perform those flying crescent and roundhouse kicks we see so much in martial arts movies, but unless you are a very highly-skilled martial artist with control, balance and perfect timing, attempts at protecting yourself with this use of your legs may work against you. If your leg is grabbed, you will be in trouble. There is a good example of this in the film *Crocodile Dundee*.

The high, flashy kicks are good exercise and fun to perform but are not necessarily the best choice in a self-defence situation. Minimal use of your legs and feet to sensitive areas of a cowardly aggressor will prove to be immediately effective. Study the following uses of your foot/leg weapons.

How to Strike

You will summon much more of the power of your full body/mind/spirit if you mentally prepare yourself to use your natural physical weapons to strike *through and beyond* your target rather than at the target.

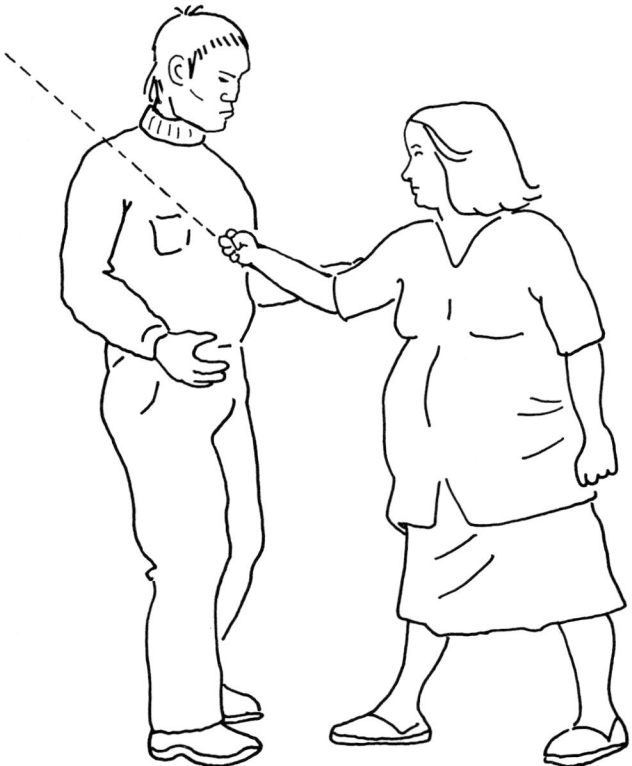

Striking and Kicking Accurately

In the following exercise you will sharpen your accuracy skills. If you practise ten minutes at least three times a week, the skill of accuracy will be yours for life.

1 Get a large piece of art or butcher paper (six feet long). Put it up on the wall and draw the body-shape and facial expression of the type of aggressor you are most afraid

of. Start by drawing the general shape then fill in the features (eyes, nose, mouth, etc).

2 Aim at each point, but keep at least an inch distance between your hand and the wall to prevent injury. Practise follow-through on your kicking and punching by using the 3-D target dummy described below. Practise using each of your weapons, keeping in mind the associated principles mentioned above. Imagine it to be a real situation with danger. Be aware of the fact that you may feel afraid, panicky and angry. When you contact your anger use it like a seething volcano inside you but try to keep a cool and focused head.

3 Notice the weapons you feel most attracted to. Work on them first. Shape the weapon through your body. Then practise striking twenty times with each one. Try to get through all the weapons so as to expand your possibilities, though bear in mind the ones that feel most natural for you.

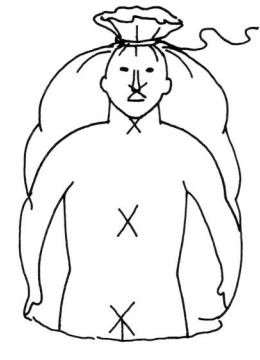

Make Your 3-D Target Dummy

It is best to develop your accuracy with a three-dimensional target. To do this you can make your own target dummy. You will need: a large burlap sack; at least two gallons of sand; some quarter-inch rope; a large marking pen; a garage, cellar or tree (for hanging the dummy).

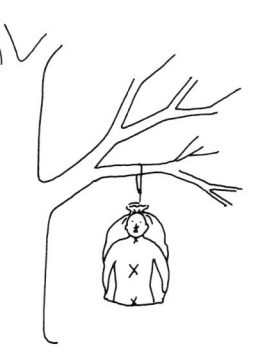

1 Using a marker pen, draw the upper body, groin and torso onto the sack, marking the most strategic vulnerable points.

2 Fill the sack with sand, tying with strong twine.

3 Make a hoop in the end of the twine to hang the dummy from a strong hook or a sturdy tree branch.

If you wish, try to find other ways to construct your own target dummy ideas.

Moving Target Practice

You can improve your accuracy with a moving target by suspending a rubber ball from a string. Do this in a safe place away from windows or other breakables.

1 With a strong piece of nylon, make a small hole through the ball and pull the elastic through. Tie a knot in the end of the string once it is through the ball to secure it. Secure the elastic to the ceiling of your garage or to a tree branch.
2 Practise using your weapons for accuracy while the ball jumps around. The smaller the ball, the greater your accuracy reflexes.
3 You can also work with three or more balls all around you at different levels so that you may practise accuracy whilst revolving as though you are dealing with more than one coward. The lower placed-balls will also allow you to practise your kicks.

Speed: A Relative Thing

Speed has always been an attraction to the world of self-defence. Being able to capture the 'blur of speed' we see so much in the martial arts movies is an attractive prospect. Other movies such as *The Karate Kid* show how even the slow pedestrian activities we do like painting, polishing and scrubbing can develop powerful movement patterns that, when mindfully executed, can be accessed with great alacrity in a self-defence situation. The authentic movements of Kung Fu (which means *functioning human*), originated out of the movement used in agricultural activities as well as in the motions expressed in calligraphy. Natural movements have greater longevity than artificially-imposed kicks and punches. For example, after pruning vines for one week I developed a strong grip which enhanced my judo mat work technique. In the film *Rocky IV*, Sylvester Stallone demonstrates how the power of training for his fight in natural ways such as in chopping wood and climbing mountains carries an advantage whose power is in the survival instinct. These movements are meaningful and practical whereas the training of his steroid-pumped opponent hooked up to all types of monitoring machinery in artificial gym settings ultimately led to his opponent's failure. Essentially the motto was: a fighter without heart cannot win.

With all of this in mind I would like to define speed as any relative action done in such a way as to accomplish the desired results. This can appear slow or fast. **The main thing to be aware of is your sense of safety.**

When does it feel safe to move? I met one of my students who had been skeptical about the practical use of the slow and deliberate movements of Chi-Kung. Frustrated, after two months of training she dropped out of class. A year later I met her at a coffee shop where she came up to me and seemed anxious to tell me something. She said that she had to let me know that a man entered her house through a partially-opened window one night in the early hours of the morning. She woke to find the cowardly man sitting upon her, pinning her under the covers, with a knife at her throat. She said that it took her some time to get over the feeling that she was dreaming. When she did, she was surprised to find that she felt angry rather than afraid. Instinctively, she used the movement she had doubted had any practical value in Chi-Kung. This involved moving the arm and shoulder back in a large circular motion and then, with the fingertips pointing forward, a sweeping scooping motion forward. The movement is almost saying that it is collecting inner strength to direct it forward. Her use of it in bed and during the attack involved her using a more concentrated and compact version of the exercise as she twisted and turned herself free. When she made this movement she threw the coward across the room back toward the window he had slimily entered, at which point he scrambled through the window as she was getting herself out of bed. Her only regret was that she couldn't catch him, but she was proud that this movement she had practised in our slow, sleepy way had meaning after all.

Like the tortoise and the hare story, slow can often prove to be fast. In classical Tai-Chi training one practises slowly for seven years before entering into the faster pace. The slow, mindful movements eventually train the student to mentally slow down a fast movement so that something that seems sudden to most people can be calibrated into slow-moving frames by the Tai-Chi practitioner. This makes for more time to respond, to get out of the way or to intercept.

Speed Training

1 It is good to get the 'blur of speed' out of your system first. Use your target balls from the accuracy training and practise hitting as fast as you can. Now see what happens when you relax your body, aim, and then reserve your speed for the moment of contact.

2 Now practise moving in slow motion to the target with your best concentration. You will know that you are concentrating in a relaxed rather than tense way when you can strike at your targets without blinking for at least thirty seconds. This is desirable.

3 Now put your training to the test with a partner as you practise your Wing Tsun defensive to offensive training (Chapter 3), exploring the efficiency of the various speeds you have practised. The feedback of your success raises your learning curve right before your eyes.

Inch Power

After you have discovered your proficient speed with accuracy, you can add another level to your safety tool chest: inch power. This is a concept that was greatly developed by Bruce Lee. It is a highly-distilled technique that allows you to concentrate the power and focus of any technique into an inch, and then to magnify the power. So that rather than delivering 150 pounds of pressure in a low kick, you can generate up to 1000 pounds of pressure to defend yourself. This is an interesting concept to explore and develop as a challenge to your training. However it is not actually necessary because, when you direct any of your physical weapons to their respective sensitive targets, you only need accuracy and intent to temporarily redirect a cowardly attacker's attention back to themselves. The best inch power comes from natural movements such as an acceleration of the way your arms swing when you are walking and the swing of your leg from your hip to be directed into a kick. You may also develop inch power by using the isometric exercise wherein you press your fist (little finger side down) into your other cupped hand. The cupped hand should then prevent the fist from pressing forward. Hold for ten seconds and repeat ten times on each side.

STRATEGIC SELF-DEFENCE AGAINST LETHAL WEAPONS

To develop confidence in basic self-defence against a coward who uses lethal weapons such as guns or knives you must first demystify these weapons by handling them so that their mere appearance doesn't throw you into a panic. Beyond this demystifying process, observe the following steps:

1 Remember the coward is more afraid of you than you need to be of them because they feel they can't handle you on their own and without the use of the weapon. If they have not shot you dead, you still have time to respond.
2 If you are trapped with a lethal weapon pointing at you, go along with the coward until you feel safe to escape.
3 Know where the line of fire is, i.e. the point and cutting-edge of the knife, the firing hole of the gun. RESPECT these dangerous parts. Move away from the line of fire or the edge of the knife. Learn through rehearsal to become comfortable with the closeness of a weapon pointing into your back or at your throat or wherever your greater fear lies.

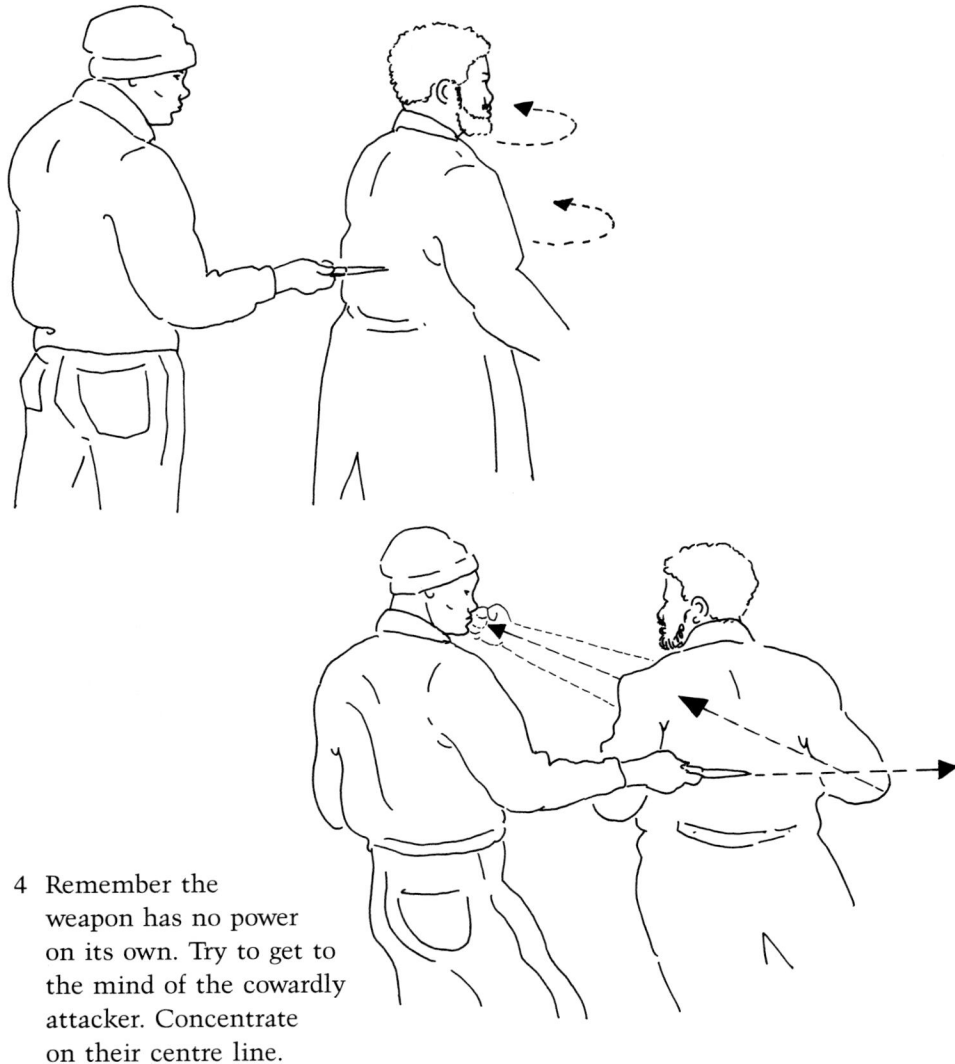

4 Remember the weapon has no power on its own. Try to get to the mind of the cowardly attacker. Concentrate on their centre line.

5 When you feel safe to move and you are *out of the line of fire*, pounce on the attacker's wrist with your hand. At the same time, strike the nose to weaken the coward so that you will not be within striking distance. Control the wrist and hand of the aggressor by locking their elbow.

6 Get the weapon from the coward and throw it as far as you can so that it cannot be readily available for them to use again as you complete your flight from the situation.

Alternatively, if they are knocked out from your strike to the nose you may take the weapon with you to turn in to the police as evidence.

YOUR POWER ANIMALS

Each of us has an animal or two that we admire or fear. Another natural and useful tool for self-defence comes from nature. This is a concept that has been used by the indigenous peoples of America and by shamans. It involves recognizing and summoning the power of the animals (and insects for that matter) you are most attracted to, or afraid of. You may have noticed that you admire the beauty and speed of a leopard, the timing of a king cobra, the grace and comfort of a swan, the peskiness of a fly. Your power animal can teach you about repressed or hidden parts of yourself that you may be afraid to express.

One of my students told me how she had used the spirit of her power animal, a tigress, to protect her from being raped on a deserted desert road. When she found herself surrounded by a gang of motorcyclists, she immediately went into tigress mode. Realizing that her self-esteem was not yet up to what she would like it to have been, she imagined that she was protecting her cubs (as she interpreted the undeveloped, yet full of potential parts of herself). She crouched down, felt the strength in her shoulders and hands and was ready to fight to the death. She said they must have sensed this because they slowed down and made some lewd comments. When she responded in this, what may appear to others to have been, crazed posture, they sped off. She knew she had succeeded.

Calling Upon the Spirit of Your Power Animal

1 Name the qualities of the animal you like and/or of the animal you fear.
2 Name the capabilities of the animal(s).
3 Sit quietly and meditatively, letting these qualities become present in you. Now imagine yourself using these abilities in a self-defence situation.
4 Notice how these qualities are within you always. Notice how they help you deal with the daily challenges of living. Keep them in the background as your lethal weapon or, in the advice of the heroic psychiatrist in an

old Bette Davis classic, *Now Voyager,* 'Aim your gun, but don't shoot until you have to.'

WEI-CHI

In the art of Chi-Kung (the oldest martial/healing art), there is a practice called wei-chi. This is the internally-strengthening, vital force that builds our immune systems and then radiates out like a magnetic, yet radiant and protective force.

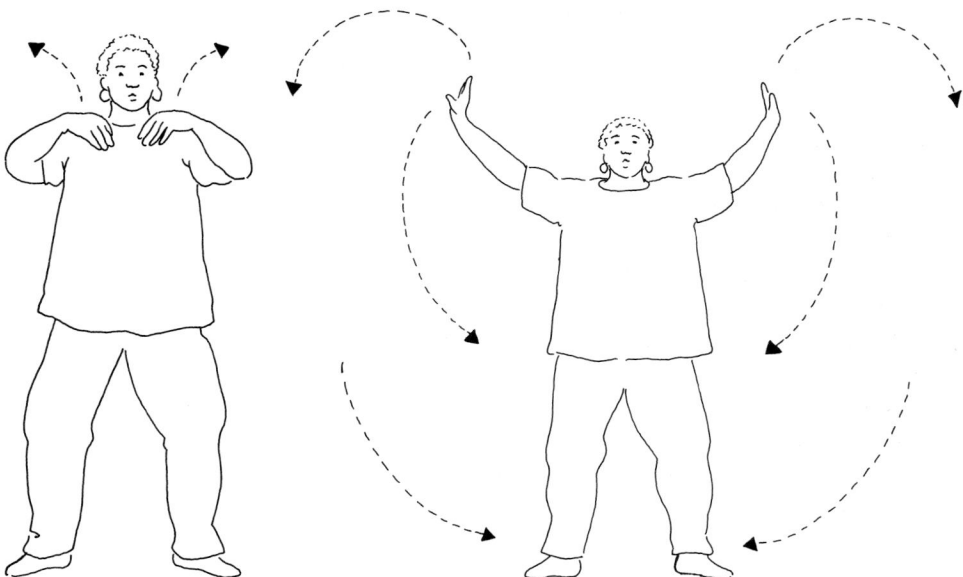

You can build your wei-chi by many means. Besides your awareness of how you have survived and overcome difficulties so far, the exercise below is an excellent place to start.

Build Your Wei-Chi

The wei-chi exercise will improve the inner and outer quality of your magnetic field. Over time you will find that your intuition will be stronger and more accurate. You will be increasingly able to be in the right place at the right time. You will also be able to detect signals in your personal relationships that are not healthy for the well-being of you or the other person(s). Once you recognize the signals you will be able to trust your timing to communicate your intentions in appropriate ways for you.

1 Stand with your feet shoulder-width apart.
2 Relax your feet, tummy, back, shoulders and face as much as possible.
3 Bend your knees slightly so that you feel a springy quality in your legs.
4 Maintain a feeling of having your feet relaxed and rooted into the earth, whilst your head is pulled up in an inspired manner above the clouds.
5 Bring your palms up to your solar plexus and inhale deeply, allowing your lower abdomen and lower back to expand with the inhalation, and then to contract with the exhalation as you direct your palms down. Repeat this for three minutes at first. Then increase your time up to twenty minutes every morning.

6 Now take some of this energy and spread it around you in a circular motion with your arms. Repeat this three times. Then turn to the two sides so that you cover front and back.

7 Finish by gathering your fingers into a fist, and then stretch your fist down toward the earth at your sides. This will help ground you in this spherical awareness and radiance.

OVERCOMING SHOCK

If you have ever been attacked mentally, physically or verbally you know how debilitating the effects of shock can be. Unless you have had the means to deal with the shock, it can remain in your body wielding its crippling effects for years until it is checked.

Shock is one of the major reasons that we lose our sense of grounding. When the body/mind goes into shock there is a dramatic tightening in the *erector spinae* muscles (long muscles along the spine); a loss of contact with the warmth in the tummy and solar plexus; cold extremities; dilation or alternatively a lack of presence in the pupils (eyes), and a disconnected feeling in the legs and feet.

The ramifications of shock in one's daily routine include constant fatigue or hyperactivity, spaciness, depression, and an inability to settle comfortably into any activity - a general inability to focus. Unchannelled shock drains one's power.

Even when one hasn't been attacked recently, the symptoms of shock can even result from a startling event in early childhood. The more sensitive the individual, the more likely they are to go into shock. Sometimes shock is useful when it catalyzes growth - that is, when one realizes what has happened and has a chance to reground comfortably into the new way of being.

First Aid for Shock or Trauma

DO NOT USE IF THE PERSON IS BLEEDING ANYWHERE IN THE ENTIRE TORSO AREA. Firmly apply pressure to acupressure points - top of the head and heart constrictor (inside middle of forearm).

Solar plexus balancing: right hand to spine, left hand to solar plexus. Feel for a pulse or pulses in your fingertips or in the person's body, and then wait for the pulse to synchronise.

Daily Preventative

1 Consciously breathe deeply for 3–5 minutes, or until you feel comfortable in your body. Try to feel the bowl of your pelvis and the base of your spine under you in a rooted way, the soles of your feet should feel warm and tingly and connected to the ground, your tummy warm, your chest open and airy, your neck long and shoulders even and relaxed. The top of your head should feel as though it is being gently suspended from a silver thread which leads to the inspirational, expansive parts of you.

2 Walk around, stamp your feet on the ground, and pay particular attention to a solid feeling in your heels. Include sound that comes from your belly as you stamp. Do this until you feel frustration and anger leave your body.

3 Learn to recognize your own shock signals. What are they? Write them down for future reference. Actually rehearse them so they become familiar to you. Find your personal route through the shock into grounding.

4 Recognize and develop your quality of well-being.

The Bear Exercise

The therapeutic Chi-Kung Bear exercise is especially strengthening to the grounding and nourishing stomach and spleen functions. Do this after you have eaten. Keep your legs stiff and lead with your full tummy. With your palms turned in toward your body, keep your arms parallel in front of you.

Do this until you feel tired and then stop the motion and observe the warm and grounding energy you have generated. Pay particular attention to the feeling in your legs and feet.

GUARDING AGAINST EMOTIONAL BLACKMAIL

One of the most subtle needs for self-defence revolves around the way we try to accomplish our goals by plugging into another person's emotional sensitivity. I'm afraid that women have allowed this nasty little bit of conditioning to infiltrate our ways of operating on a daily level. I am referring to the times we resort to comments such as, 'Don't be selfish and think of your dreams; think of your husband and children.' This also happens on a cultural and religious level when we have been brought up with the controlling guillotine of guilt and fear. When we allow these autocratic rulers to push us around there is little room left for us to be direct, clear and upfront with our intentions. The use of hidden agendas becomes the common mode of expression.

To some of us, being direct can seem arrogant and even blasphemous. I remember being removed from the congregation of the southern baptists church many times. One occasion sticks in my memory: the preacher during his sermon had let us know that we are deeply loved by God. I liked this because like most of us, I enjoy being loved. But I could not cope with the preacher's comment which came later with reverberating emphasis: 'So you must fear the Lord.' At this point I popped up out of my seat and inquired in an equally loud voice in front of God and everyone: 'But if God loves us, why should we be afraid?' Out of church I was quickly snatched, and without my answer, I might add! Later, I came to the conclusion that this type of logic must be at the root of some of the other related comments listed below:

'I love you, that's why I am beating you.'
'You know I will die soon, so you should be here with me.'
'You know we are all women trying to get ahead, so why don't you give money to this cause?' (Sometimes 'this cause' ends up being a scam.)
'You women will never get ahead until you help liberate the whole race.'

'I know I chose to have the child but the whole neighbourhood should be responsible for it.'

'If you loved me you would ——'.

'You're a black woman so you should pay for a sister to get ahead.'

'Don't get angry. It doesn't become you.'

'How can you talk to me and your father this way when we pay for your meals and clothes?'

Emotional blackmail is a result of people feeling powerless. It works by combining the ingredients of an emotional issue with something that is desired and making a manipulative cocktail. Emotional blackmail is the major 'tool of the trade' for conmen and women. It does not help the perpetrators to gain power, though, when we appease this common form of manipulation. If you let it motivate you it can leave lasting emotional scars because your heart will know that you were manipulated. It will also leave you open to be manipulated in this way in the future.

The best way that I know to deal with this blackmail is to educate ourselves through awareness, and to name it when we see it in others: 'You are using emotional blackmail and I will not respond to it.' You can follow it with: 'Are you aware that you are using emotional blackmail?' Then you can explain what it is, if you choose.

Emotional blackmail is a subtle form of rape. It is disempowering. Like dealing with a rapist, it is only by confronting it that we can defuse its humiliating and destructive power.

COMMUNITY INTERVENTION: BEATING THE RAPIST

In addition to teaching Judo at the University of California at Santa Cruz, I taught self-defence for Women Against Rape (WAR). This was a very valuable experience for me in many ways. It was particularly satisfying to work with a dedicated group of women who were committed to strategically dealing with the major sources and ramifications that contribute to and reinforce the rapist's behaviour. The most outstanding theme of WAR is to help women take back their power after the disempowering fallout of rape. They successfully achieve this with listening, counselling and providing self-defence classes.

One of the most satisfying things we did together was to confront the rapist. The rationale addressed the fact that the criminal justice system does not really change the motives of the cowardly rapist. In fact 80 per cent of the men who are convicted of rape do it again when they leave prison. It seems that their stay in prison only serves to provide more sophisticated rape tactics.

Many rapists are known in a community. They continue to rape because women and children are afraid to speak out. Even those who do find the strength and courage to do so are punished again in the courts when it seems that they, the victims, are put on trial rather than the rapist.

Because of this lack of sensibility in the criminal justice system, WAR provides a comforting alternative for women and children who have been raped. Back in the late 1970s we confronted the rapists we knew about from the women who had been attacked. We would find his address through various methods. This was intended to support the woman in regaining her power. She was always given the choice to be at the scene of the confrontation or to stay behind and later receive our reports of what happened.

Before embarking upon the confrontation we would meet sometimes several times to discuss when we would approach the man, who would be the first spokeswoman, who would grab his arms, legs, etc. should he become violent, and who would carry the camera and snap (with flash) the photos of the man. Then we would contact Men Against Rape (MAR) to have them follow us in these very public places, to let any bystanders know what was going on, to distribute leaflets to the crowd about what we were doing, and then to offer the man counselling after we completed the confrontation; as you can imagine it was quite a scene.

In these situations we found ourselves confronting men at their homes in front of their wives and children, in their offices, in restaurants where they were working and at the university. Some people are surprised to find that most rapists are known by the woman and some are apparently upstanding citizens.

The confrontation would begin with us entering the premises where the cowardly man was. When he appeared we would say in very strong voices:

'_____ , we are here because you raped _____ on _____ . We want you to know that we know who you are and where you are, and soon the whole community will. We believe her. You are not crazy. You must change your attitude toward women and toward yourself. We expect you to change!

If the woman who was raped was present we would make sure that he listened to what she had to say. The reaction of the man was of great surprise. Sometimes they would wet their pants or defecate on the spot; they were so shocked. This was part of our strategy. We wanted to educate them about how it feels to have your privacy aggressively interrupted, to feel afraid, and to not be able to speak. In some situations the man would try to verbally deny that he had done anything. When he did we would interrupt him by saying that it was not his time to speak. He had to listen.

These confrontations are very effective because they not only destroy the abuser's anonymity (his greatest survival crutch) by removing him from hiding behind often unfortunate, romantic media titles, such as 'The Ripper'. This teaches him that he is a human being who is being watched by the community and he is expected to change.

Such confrontations are empowering to all the women and children who witness them. I will never forget one confrontation with a preacher who had raped one of the members of his congregation who had come to him for counselling. When the woman spoke up during the confrontation saying that, contrary to what he thought, she did not like it, her young daughter turned the heads of all who were listening when she piped up with: 'Yeah, and I didn't like it when you did it to me either.'

When some people hear about these confrontations they ask if we aren't just being being vigilantes, taking the law into our own hands. Perhaps we are. I like to take the meaning of the word at face value and say it is about being vigilant. The bonus is that the offender, the rapist, is hearing about his actions on a very human level. Many have reported to their counsellors that they didn't realize they had really caused pain. They thought they were just being *manly*. My brother comically describes this type of mentality as 'a man with a severe problem with his testosterone levels'.

The more the community gets involved rather than just waiting for the criminal justice system to respond, the quicker we will clean out rape and other forms of abuse. One elderly woman believes that, if more grandmothers would claim back the streets at night, rather than huddling fearfully and helplessly in their homes, there would be fewer attacks. Some men I have spoken with believe that a man who rapes should be gang-raped. Still other men and women believe that the rapist should have his penis removed. I believe that the rapist should be treated as what he or she is – an emotionally-disturbed child who needs clear and direct communication with very firm boundaries. And until they grow up emotionally and in their actions they should be watched very closely by the community. The government could address the abusers by setting up therapeutic facilities wherein they are required to witness the anger of the one(s) they have abused. This would be followed by skilled counselling and a strong expectation for the abuser to grow in self-esteem and, as a consequence, have more respect for others. When the community gets involved it helps educate people so that domestic violence and abuse will be abated too.

SUMMARY AND SAFETY TIPS

Attempted rape

1 Remember, no matter how imposing this person is, somewhere they are very weak. This is why they have to lower themselves to such a cowardly act. Remember they have vulnerable areas; if they are masked and padded, you can try talking to them. You may have to wait until it feels safe for you to retaliate and escape. Trust your intuition about people who don't feel right and move away to prevent attack.

2 Get your pelvis under you and feel the power in your vagina, your anus, your breast. I remember a scene from a Diana Ross film called *Mahogany*. She was being followed by a slimy little man in an alleyway. Instead of cowering, she turned to face him, thrust her pelvis forward and said: 'Here, you want it? You want some p___y?' She continued to thrust her pelvis at him in the most 'unladylike' fashion until he ran off, horrified at such a sight. We need to reclaim the power in this

part of ourselves as women. Our life-giving genitals have been turned into cursed parts of us. The power we have in this area is so feared by some men that they have mutilated our genitalia so that some of us cannot have access to this power. Use this power to fuel your body's innate ability to defend you. Your sexual energy can be used creatively and instinctively to respond to situations in appropriate ways for you.

Date rape

Your self-esteem is ultimately your best protection in dating situations as it will help you select people who are appropriate for you. Before you go out with someone you don't know well, prepare yourself by checking in with your emotional and physical motives. Why are you going out with this person? What are you willing to do with them? Where and how will you draw the line if they want to do something that doesn't feel right to you? How will you clearly communicate this to them? Where are your escape routes? Who are your allies or potential allies in your dating environment?

Walking

Make sure you walk with the correct body language. What are you communicating in your walk? Walk tall so that you can breathe and move more efficiently. This will maximize your intuition. Allow your eyes to feel full the way they do right before you drop off to sleep so that you are more relaxed in your perceptions and your peripheral vision increases.

If you sense that someone is following you, cross the road to find out if you are correct, or alter your speed to see if it has any effect on the suspected person. Turn around and either watch them from head to toe, or say something to them. You may also walk into a public place.

Reacting to 'Innocent' Requests

When a stranger asks you the time, immediately take a step away from them so that you can keep a full view of their body. If they move closer to you, move away again while you answer them. If they continue to follow you, you will know that their intent is more aggressive than simply asking the time. At this point you may have to employ whichever tactic you feel is appropriate.

Driving, and Leaving Parked Cars

1 When you suspect someone is following you, work out the nearest, most public place and drive there even if it is off your route.
2 Lock your doors so that someone cannot jump into your car at red lights.
3 Park in well-lit places.
4 Check your car before you get in to make sure no one has entered and is laying in waiting for you.
5 When you park your car, be sure to remove personal belongings such as purses, combs, make-up, women's shoes. These belongings can broadcast to a would-be cowardly attacker that you are a woman.

When Travelling to Other Cities or Countries

1 Be sure to learn about the area that you will be staying. Which crimes tend to occur there (such as professional child pickpockets in Florence, Italy)? Which diseases exist there? How can you take precautionary measures? What is the climate and food situation? Are you likely to be vulnerable in this climate? How can you make yourself less vulnerable? Do you know the language?
2 Be aware, if you are suffering from jet lag, and do not make any hasty decisions, especially where business is concerned. Have some knowledge of the language, or travel with someone who does.
3 Keep your body language especially alert when you are walking in an unfamiliar area, especially with jet lag.

4 Unless you are with a cohesive group, avoid carrying cameras and foreign equipment and clothes to let would-be attackers know you are a tourist.

Watch for Men Disguised as Disabled People or as Little Old Ladies

Pay particular attention to people who try to solicit your sympathy, such as little old ladies in parking lots or men who appear to be charming and disabled. I know of two situations where rapists have disguised themselves as *little old women* in parking lots who approach women for rides when they come out of the stores with their shopping.

Ted Bundy, one of the most vicious serial killers, approached and seduced one of his victims into his twisted, fatal web, by masquerading as a charming, handsome young student on crutches who needed help in a college parking lot. When he received the sympathy he was plotting for, he violently attacked and murdered the young woman with his crutches.

Women Living Alone

Cowardly attackers often look for homes that have an air of vacancy about them. Set up your environment so that it is full of you: colours, objects you like should be around you. This is a reflection of your self-esteem. Make a point of going into each room and filling it with your presence. Be sure to check doors and windows before leaving and upon entering. Know who your allies are in the neighbourhood. Make an emergency list of allies you could call upon if you need them because sometimes we can't think of those people when we are under the stress of, for example, a burglary.

Advice of Doctors

Many of us know the importance of seeking two or more opinions before having any form of surgery. Make sure that you also know your doctor's attitude, if they have prejudice toward you as a woman, or your cultural background, or to what you are doing as a woman. I have encountered such prejudice in the complementary medical fields, especially with Asian male doctors whose attitudes suggest that something is wrong with me for doing the work I do. Some believe a woman is only healthy when she is at home and having babies.

When dealing with practitioners in complementary medicine, make sure they are skilled in the mechanics of their field. I can't tell you how irritating it has been going to people for a massage and being a target for their need to play psychiatrist, when all I wanted was to have a relaxing therapeutic massage.

Helping to Prevent Children Becoming Abusers

1 Be as clear and honest with your children as possible. Children know what is going on all around them even though they may not yet have the language to talk about it. Be straight with them when something isn't going right. They are more resilient than we think, especially when they know that your intentions are to let them know what is going on. Increasingly, there seems to be a link between secrets kept from young children, especially about their fathers' identity, with violent dispositions later in life.

2 The more children experience violence the more likely they are to seek the balance by being violent when they are more powerful adults, or by becoming violent to themselves.

3 Try to avoid dumping your fears on to them. Let them know that you are there to protect and take care of them. Then tell them what you will or will not allow when you are in the role of their guardian. Teach them to discriminate who is dangerous from who is not, rather than covering them with morality blankets such as 'respect your elder's at all costs'.

4 Treat them with respect, as the intelligent, feeling people they are. Ask them questions. Keep their minds

working so that they get the feedback that what they have to say is important. Ask them about how their day went so that you can pick up cues about whether they have been bullied or are being the playground bullies.

5 Plan parenthood so that you know your child will have a better chance for a strong, safe and happy life.

Wise Ones Over 60

Do not succumb to the unfortunate arrogant attitudes that make you feel redundant. Claim back the wisdom and strength that has come from your long life and make it work for you. Collectively amass the momentum of your wishes and present them to your governing bodies. Make them create jobs and programmes that will honour us with the wisdom of your experience.

Keep yourself fit. All of that wisdom put into a healthy, fit body will be the best example to all that being older can be a great treasure.

Neighbours

Set up a neighbourhood watch scheme to protect your neighbourhood. Cowardly, desperate people can sense when there is a unified awareness and they will be less likely to target a neighbourhood where people are watching out for each other.

Combined Technique

Explore using a combination of techniques to improve your versatility.

OVERVIEW

Safety begins at home. Make sure that you have taken sensible security measures such as window locks, double bolts and well-lit entrance areas.

Set up your immediate environment so that it reflects and reinforces your self-esteem and will provide an emotional base of security when you are out in the world.

CHECKLIST

☑ **Protective Instincts** If you find yourself under attack, use your protective instincts, like those of a maternal animal, in ways that you feel comfortable.

☑ **Flight Distance** Wherever you are, at home, walking near an alleyway, at work or in a new area, make sure that you have flight distance.

☑ **Drug/Alcohol Abuse** Eighty per cent of domestic and public violence is caused by substance abuse. Learn the signals of drug and alcohol abuse as a way of precluding potential aggression by establishing your 'flight distance' and by finding ways to enhance your self-esteem. This will help you to effectively cope with the realities of the situation. You may need outside support for this.

☑ **Accuracy** Remember that when you are under pressure to defend yourself physically the quality and potency of your response depends on your being accurate. Know the attacker's vulnerable points, especially the nose, eyes, throat and groin.

☑ **Your Natural Weapons** Rather than relying on guns, knives, mace, etc, develop your natural weapons through practice, as outlined in this chapter, so that they will be there for you if you need them. Always practise in the spirit of danger. Work with your fears and anger by channelling them into your practice.

☑ **Speed** Remember speed is relative to safety. Move quickly when you can safely do so.

☑ **Community Allies** Know who your allies are along any routes that you frequent whether it be on your way to work, a holiday visit or the route to your friend's house. Know who you can call upon for help should you need them.

☑ **Safety Tips** Observe general safety tips as outlined in this chapter, especially by developing wei-chi.

AFFIRMATION

I maintain my safety by making decisions that are based on my most important values.

5 | The Fifth Dimension

THE REALM OF HAPPINESS

Out of knowing what you can do mentally and physically comes confidence. Out of confidence comes decisive action. Out of action comes manifestation. Out of manifestation comes joy or sadness.

To conclude our journey into the comprehensive world of self-defence we will investigate tools for strengthening the very 'emotional content' that motivates our daily actions around confidence and vulnerability.

If intent is the light we feed ourselves, then emotional security is the water. The result of a healthy self-defence programme is a happier person. In this chapter we will look at the foundations of our emotional security to determine how far it is possible to take the concepts and skills presented in this book.

We come full circle now as we journey across the bridge between some of the innermost parts of ourselves, such as our emotional/spiritual make-up, and the ways we may constructively manifest these as inner motives. In this way, we will see that reclaiming the mechanisms that fuel our sense of purpose is the best form of self-defence.

I will introduce this chapter by establishing common ground. I refer to the meaning in *Webster's New World Dictionary*:

Happy 1. lucky, fortunate; 2. having, showing, or causing great pleasure or joy; 3. suitable and clever, apt.

But what does this have to do with self-defence? you may ask.

In the research that precipitated my writing of *Stand Your Ground*, I found a consistent deficit in the approaches to the topic of self-defence: Aimed at women as victims they were all iambic and, though sometimes humorous, they were not very poetic. 'Don't walk out at night. Lock your doors and windows. Don't wear provocative clothes. And if you do have to walk at all, carry a hat pin.'! As I see it the error in this approach lies in the fact that the emphasis is on defence and not on the self.

Flipping through the standard card catalogues I found the first entries under the topic of defence to be *national defence* and *defence mechanisms*. I am quite sure the advice mentioned above was given with good will to address swiftly and responsibly threats of violence to the nation as a whole. It was not, however, thought out in terms of a strategy to set into motion educational sources that would address and combat the very causes of violence, thus minimizing the need for self-defence. Through the complex web of causes for violence there is a basic truth: when a person is not happy, especially as a child, they strike out in anger. As we saw in the last chapter, much violence centres around drug abuse. People in pain take something to enable them to escape it and then they become numb to their own sense of purpose and that of others. Human life loses its value.

STEPPING OUT OF THE VICTIM/ATTACKER SYNDROME

Much of the frustration that leads to aggressive and chronic victim behaviour stems from the individual's attempts to conform to socially acceptable qualities, expression of those qualities and the pursuit of social and career goals that reflect those qualities. Deeper than racial and class prejudice, the fundamental division in what is right and what is wrong with a person comes down to what gender the person is. This assignment of what one can and cannot do based on gender is a short-sighted and flawed imposition on the true potential of the individual.

We step out of the role of victim when we claim back ourselves, when we celebrate the uniqueness of our different features as well as what we have in common with others in our human qualities; when we stop being motivated solely by what is expected of us and replace it with what we know is important to us; when we find ways to heal ourselves back to the pleasurable and happy state we were intended to occupy; when we honour the strengths and beauty of our different heritages without comparing ourselves to other races; when we initiate constructive positive action around the colour of our skin; when we recognize how we have survived so far and build upon these survival skills, using them to mobilize us into more fulfilling lives. When we claim back ourselves we find that we are a combination of uniqueness and the common threads we share with all humanity. When we do this we release the ignorance and arrogance that leads us to believe that we are separate from and controlling of nature. Once we get in touch with what is most meaningful to each of us, we muster the resources needed to learn from our painful experiences and then to protect ourselves in the most appropriate ways. We learn to express ourselves within the rules of society and culture and, more importantly, to make those rules work for us.

THE ROLE OF THE MEDIA

The media is a powerful educational tool. Too often, we hear about the most sensational, gory stories rather than the more prevalent success stories. The cowardly, emotionally-sick abusers are given Hollywood titles which surely must attract and reinforce this imbalanced way of using power. All of us who have access to radio, television and publishing should take it upon ourselves to use the media to make people aware of what is happening in the good areas as well as the bad. We should take the lead and show hope for reform in all of our societal systems where corruption and abuse prevail. We cannot wait for big brother media to do this for us. We have to take the lead.

YOUR PERSONAL NATURE REVEALED IN YOUR FINGERPRINTS

The Best Use of Your Energy

In my research via teaching, counselling and living, I have found that at the root of much personal pain and abuse are the expectations which come with gender. As a girl you should act, think, etc. in a certain way. As a boy you should act, think, not emote, etc. in a certain way. Some of these should fit some of the time. But mostly they are distracting us from being who we really are. It is all right to be presented with a list of social skills such as nurturing, being intelligent, athletic, poetic, hard, and so on, but when they are forced upon us we learn to wear emotional clothes that don't necessarily fit.

Deep within the ancient martial healing art of Chi-Kung, or QiQong, there is a system that works with the lines in our hands and our fingerprints. Depending on how it is taught the art of Chi-Kung can be one of the most empowering tools for self-knowledge. So powerful a tool for self-knowledge and empowerment, that it was banned during the cultural revolution in the 1960s. Chi-Kung is based on the philosophy of Taoism, or balance. The two major forces that act upon our bodies, our thoughts and our emotions are the receptive, nurturing and enduring *yin*, and the giving, expressive, expanding *yang*. When we have these forces balanced in ourselves and our lives, the *qi*, or vital life force, flows in every part of us. It is said that when these forces are in balance one is able to penetrate and receive the answers to life's mysteries.

Unfortunately, these forces have been misguided into the categories of gender. There are two major types of fingerprints that describe the best use of our energy (the meaning of martial arts). The wavy, swirling one is yin, which means that activity centred around a receptive, nurturing and enduring nature will be fulfilling.

Yin   Yang   Combination

The fingerprint that is depicted by a series of concentric ovals suggests that the best use of energy will be in a direct, warrior-like, giving manner.

There are also combination prints.

The system looks at all of the prints on the fingers to come up with a comprehensive map of the individual's energetic map. We may, however, approach this system strategically to find the best use of our energy out in the world. This may give you a sense of how you should best nurture and defend yourself. Look at the print on your left middle finger tip. Is it yin or yang, or a combination?

If it is yin, the area of life that you want to be involved in is to do with nurturing, being receptive, connecting people to things as well as to other people who will support your cause. You use your feelings and intuition as an instrument for understanding others.

If your fingerprint is yang, the area of life that best supports your nature is that of giving inspiration through initiating activities and structures that will make your mark in life. Any area that engages your warrior spirit will be suitable for you. You use your body and mind as an instrument for your work. This describes your most personal interests and how they may be expressed out in the world.

Now look at the fingerprint on your right middle finger. This shows the most potent way for you to express yourself and the area you discovered on the left middle finger print out in the world. So you may have a yin left middle finger which indicates that you feel at home in any field that is nurturing, that helps people, plants or animals grow into their potential; and yang on your right middle finger. The combination suggests that you can feel the strength of your energy and passion in the nurturing areas and yet, when you communicate about this it is in a yang, or more directly individual way. A combination on either or both fingers reflects an interest in areas that have a balanced blend of both yin and yang such as in music, art and justice.

The intensity and clarity of the print says something too. Strong, clear prints are feedback for a strong, clear and conscious use of your energy. If your fingerprint is faint, it shows that you may be either new to this yin or yang expression or that you are expressing it in a timid way. You can gain strength in this area by one of two ways:

1　You can immerse yourself in activities that are outlined in the nature of your fingerprint so that you are applying yourself physically and emotionally in the correct areas.
2　You can find more strength and balance by putting yourself into situations that are directly opposed to those suggested by your fingerprint. By working with your polar opposite you can enhance the clarity of your innate nature.

Your Sexuality

I recently read an article by a lesbian who described her disgust at being heavily pursued by a heterosexual man. The story goes on to describe how he thought he could convert her, yet he was attracted to her because of her strength of conviction to her sexual orientation. The shocking conclusion to her story revealed how this very man had surgically become a woman and was now the head of a lesbian organization.

There are many such stories of people trying to be something they are not and putting other people down because they are being who they really are. So much psychological and emotional conflict is the result of people trying to fit into societally-assigned gender roles that are too rigid and unrealistic. Working with your middle fingerprints can be a useful tool for cultivating the happiness that comes from being in the appropriate stream for our innate expression. Men may find that they have been fighting a nurturing nature, and women, a more direct and warrior-like spirit. When we fight our nature we fragment our vital force. This will only lead us down the path of becoming a victim or abuser in life.

YOUR NOT-SO-MYSTICAL POWER CENTRES

You may have heard of the *chakras* from the tantric and Indian yogic tradition. These points are energy vortices that relate to nerve centres and their corresponding organs and areas of the body. They can also be used to organize our awareness of how we are utilizing our energy on a personal level and out in the world. There are hundreds of them (144 in each of our hands alone). However, the most basic and classical ones are focused around seven centres.

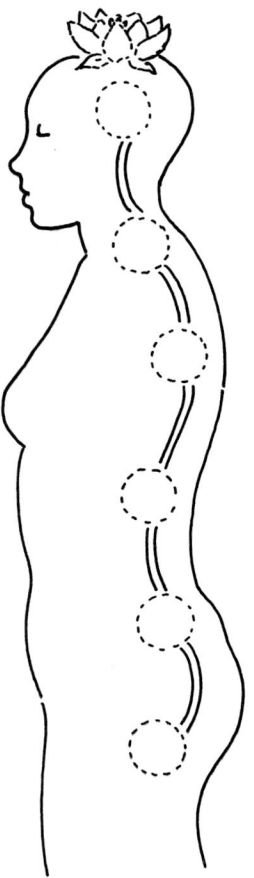

These are the chakras we will concentrate on for developing a sense of self as a basis for self-preservation. Once an idea makes its way from our heads to be accepted by the emotional self and our belief systems, it begins to resonate in the body to attract its support in becoming manifest. The idea which has become feeling enters the base of the spine at the root chakra. Depending on the idea, it either strengthens or weakens this area. The root chakra provides the foundation for the quality of interaction with the other chakras, until it finds its way into the consciousness of the crown, or self-realization.

1 The root centre controls the base of the spine, the legs and feet and our connection with the earth. This centre houses our creativity and survival abilities. If an idea coincides with the fulfilment of our purpose on earth, we feel connected and strengthened. The negative quality associated with this area is greed.

2 Once the vibration of the idea becomes rooted it travels up to the second chakra. Here is the area of emotional interaction with the yin/yang balance inside us and the way we relate emotionally to other people. It is also connected with the expression of our sexual energies. This has to do with our ability to keep emotionally balanced and to discriminate our own emotions from those around us. The negative association is excessive lust.

3 Once the vibration of the idea has been implemented on the emotional level it moves up to the third chakra

where intellectual will comes in. At this stage, awareness of how the idea is different and unique comes into consciousness and one works to structure it in such a way that it will survive. Sometimes this awareness invites opposition as the idea begins to stretch the boundaries of what seems possible. This can bring up the issue of whether we feel in or out of control of a situation. We find that to be successful and in control we have to identify ways of carrying through the idea that will be recognizable and acceptable to the rules of our family, culture and society at large. This is the area of focus, stamina and concentration; the area where everything seems to speed up. There is a quickening. The negative association with this area is over-competitiveness.

4   When the idea vibrates through this level of focus it enters the heart or the fourth chakra. This is a great leap as the idea goes from 'how can I make this work for me', to 'how does this idea contribute to the harmony and balance of everyone including nature'. Here we *feel* the idea as it is resonating in our hearts. The level of balance that was achieved in the 2nd chakra finds its impact on the balance of how we relate to our immediate and extended community environments. The negative association with this area is loneliness and over-empathy.

5   When the vibration of the idea is integrated in the heart it moves up into the throat chakra: here it becomes magnetic when we speak. On this level the idea can both attract to it what it needs to survive and repel whatever may impede its survival. This is the centre through which we express the strength of our wei-chi; the area through which we manifest the personality of all the ideas we have accepted to be true for us. The negative association for this level is lying and deception, to oneself and to others.

6   The vibration of the idea finds its place in time and space at the vision centre. Here we become conscious

of where the idea came from (perhaps even from other times) and where it is going. The negative association with this centre is cynicism.

7 The journey of the idea culminates at the crown or seventh chakra. It is at this level that we realize our destinies and, having stacked on the foundation of the other centres, we flow with the purpose of the idea vibration with revelation and joy. It is at this level that we contribute the purpose of our unique features to the world. The negative association with this centre is spaciness and disorientation.

You can work with this model of the chakras in the context of self-defence/self-preservation by applying their meaning to you and by noticing which ideas you let into your mind and, even more importantly, which ideas you begin to believe. Our ideas are very powerful. They affect our relationship with our bodies and have ramifications in the way people relate to us. If you believe you are destined to be a victim in any way because of age, gender, skin colour, class, etc. then you will unwittingly set up a chain of vibrations leading to events that support this belief.

In the following simple exercise you can strengthen your relationship with your power centres. Over time you will see how they operate. They are your employees: make them work for you. You may notice something happening in some of them. One may feel stronger than others. What is this telling you about yourself and the things you believe in?

A Treatment for Contacting and Balancing the Flow of Energy to the Chakras
You may do this lying down, sitting or standing.

1 Place the palm of your right hand on the base of your spine and your left palm above your genital area (A). Hold this area until you feel it full of warmth and fullness. You might also feel warmth and tingling in your legs and feet, a general feeling of being connected.

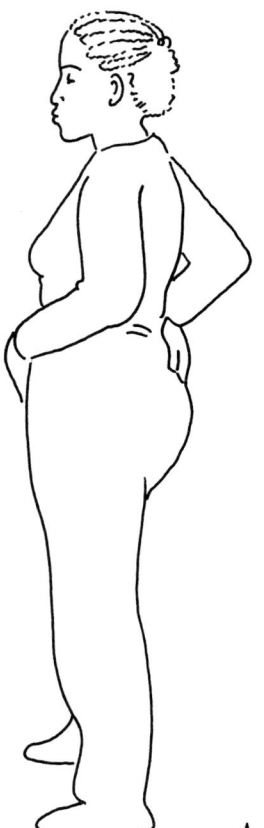

A

2 Moving up from your base centre, do this same application for each chakra by keeping your right hand on your spine behind the area and your left in front (B). When you get to your crown, place your right palm on your head and cover it with your left palm (C). After you have treated your crown, refer back to the wei-chi exercise in the last chapter to spread the awareness you have gained inside to form a radiant, protective sphere around you. Fill the sphere with your presence.

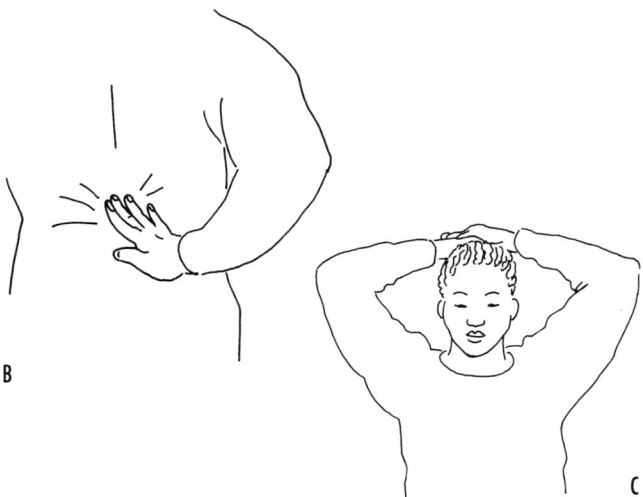

Do this treatment for yourself in the morning before getting out of bed or when you first stand up after waking. You may also do it before going to sleep. Enjoy the confident quality, the radiance and power this can bring. Notice how you attract more of the right people, places and things into your life.

CONCLUSION

The driving force behind self-defence is self-esteem. Understanding the mechanics of what makes a victim and what makes an attacker or abuser is a way to both develop and enhance how good we feel about ourselves. Beyond the obvious protective aspect of self-defence as a response to life-threatening situations, the overriding application on a daily level is truly a response to the maintenance of one's self-esteem.

With the daily reports of violence, rape, murder and the atrocities of war ever on the increase it is· easy and tempting to glaze over, to become numb and accept these unnecessary actions as part and parcel of living. I would like to appeal to a very basic part of us, to go underneath the messages we may have incorporated which cast us into positions that breed a sense of powerlessness, to go to that place of knowing where we may still have a vague memory/fantasy of the possibility of a happy and prosperous life.

Look into that place inside you, feel it, listen to it. This will become the seed, the foundation of your self-protective instinct. It always has been there and it always will be. By bringing it more to the forefront of our awareness we can give it a stronger voice. It's like bringing out an old hat – one you know has always been there: even though you don't wear it every day, it is still a part of you, no matter how recessed into the background it may seem.

Just like that old hat, the part of you that feels you are entitled to be awake, strong, confident, safe and happy, to be prosperous in appropriate ways for you and for those you love, can be donned at will at any moment to provide a new experience within an old repetitive situation. This old hat may seem a superficial prop, but it can be just the ticket for putting back a spark of confidence and warmth into your day. It can give you the inspiration to tackle areas you've put off. This may be just the catalyst you need to set the momentum of your self-esteem into motion. Once you do, look out world!

As we become more confident to pursue the things that are meaningful to us, we become more radiant, we are able to reach out to others to gain help where we need it. This is the way to a safer life.

I personally will be approaching various heads of state to encourage them to take seriously and to implement widespread programmes of education which will address the issues presented in this book. I hope you will do the same.

When enough of us implement these methods and take appropriate action by working together, then the combination of a professional approach with the weight of public opinion must have an impact on government policy and the very mechanics of *national defence* will take on a more personal and immediate meaning.

OVERVIEW

Healthy self-esteem is essential to be able to protect yourself. At some point in our lives, all of us encounter pressure from others to be what they want us to be rather than that which we truly are. When we are comfortable with ourselves we telegraph to others that they can feel comfortable with us as well as with themselves.

One of the highest levels of training comes in Chi Kung, the oldest martial art, comes when one is able to create an atmosphere of warmth, beauty, humour and love wherever one is. This is the most advanced use of one's martial (or most focussed intention) art. Staying true to oneself is the seed for the best self-defence.

CHECKLIST

- ☑ **Media** View all media (newspapers, radio, TV and film) with a critical mind and a detached point of view.
- ☑ **Gender and Race** Do not let your race or gender be a deterrent when striving to fulfil your dreams.
- ☑ **Identity** Your fingerprints, particularly those of your middle fingers, hold the key to your innate potential.

AFFIRMATION

I remain true to myself. I put into action the best of my mind, heart and body.

Best wishes to you.